Luke Prodromou
Lucia Bellini

FLASH on
English for
COMMERCE

Contents

What is Business English?

In a short time you may be studying Business English at school. But do you know exactly what it is?

1 Read the questionnaire below and tick (✓) the best answers for you.

	Yes	No	Don't know
Business English:			
1 is a list of words that are used in finance and commerce.	☐	☐	☐
2 is a language used in banking.	☐	☐	☐
3 refers to economic issues.	☐	☐	☐
4 is useful when you work with English-speaking people.	☐	☐	☐
5 is the language used in written correspondence.	☐	☐	☐
6 is useful if you want to find a job abroad.	☐	☐	☐
7 includes all aspects of buying and selling.	☐	☐	☐
8 is the language used in marketing.	☐	☐	☐
9 is important to understand economic issues.	☐	☐	☐
10 requires a good knowledge of basic grammar.	☐	☐	☐

You can answer 'Yes' to every question in the questionnaire above.
Simply speaking, Business English is the language used in international trade. In other words, it involves everything related to buying and selling. But it involves much more. Of course the starting point is the language, so you must know grammar quite well, but vocabulary can be very specific because it depends on the topic: economy, finance, products, and so on.
Business English will develop all your language skills:
■ reading (documents, texts)
■ writing (emails, reports, documents)
■ listening (conversations, presentations)
■ speaking (conversations, presentations)

These are all communication skills that you will use in business situations: when you work in your office, when you are at a meeting, when you look for information, when you take decisions related to your job.
Also, Business English will help you connect many subjects that you study at school: Economics, Finance/Accounting, Legal Studies, Geography, and also IT, and other foreign languages.

2 What other school subjects do you think you study these topics in? Write the name of the subject and check at the bottom of the page.

1 writing emails _____
2 payment methods _____
3 business legislation in the European Union _____
4 logistics and transport _____
5 different types of economic systems _____
6 writing a CV _____

1 IT   2 Finance/Accounting   3 Legal Studies   4 Geography   5 Economics   6 Foreign languages

In this book you will meet some basic and traditional Business English topics.

3 **Complete the table of topics with a description of the topic contents from the list below.**

Content:
- Money is the driving force in business. Banks, profits, sales are key words.
- An enterprise that sells or buys goods or services. It must be organized into departments with different activities.
- The place where goods and services are bought and sold. The people involved are producers, sellers, consumers.
- There is a set of laws regulating international business that must be followed. Working in the business world also implies being able to understand and prepare documents like contracts, payment and transport documents, invoices, and others.
- The process of buying and selling. It consists of personal contact, speaking over the phone, writing emails, preparing documents, sending goods, solving problems.
- Today all companies must beat competition if they want to sell their product. This means that they must be good at producing the right product, at the right price and persuading people to buy it.
- Looking for and finding a job in a foreign country. It means writing and speaking about your qualifications and skills.

	Topic	Content
	The market	
	The company	
	Business transactions	
	The job market	
	Business documents and legislation	
	Finance	
	Marketing	

2 The Market

A market is where people buy and sell. The people who sell are called sellers – also producers or manufacturers – they make and provide what the market needs. The people who buy are called buyers – also customers – they use what they buy from sellers. But what is bought and sold in a market? Goods and services. Goods are physical objects like computers, mobile phones, shoes, spaghetti. Services are non-physical objects like banking, transport, concerts, advertising. Of course the quantity and type of goods and services produced interacts with the quantity and type of goods and services the market demands. This is called the law of supply and demand. The supply is the quantity of goods or services that producers put in the market. Demand is the amount of goods and services that buyers will buy. Producers make what consumers require because they don't want to produce something that nobody wants to buy. This law is the driving force of any market. But what influences a customer's choice of what product to buy and in what quantity? One of the most important factors that determines this choice is the price. In general, people buy more when the price is low and buy less when it is high. This can create competition in the market between different sellers of the same product who want to win as many customers as possible, so they must beat competitors but, at the same time, they must make a profit.

1 Match these words with their definitions.

1 producer
2 customer
3 services
4 market
5 price
6 supply and demand
7 goods
8 advertising

a ☐ A place where buyers and sellers are in contact with one another.
b ☐ The relationship between the quantity of products and services that are for sale and the quantity that people want to buy.
c ☐ A company or person that makes goods.
d ☐ Things produced and sold.
e ☐ Someone who buys goods or services.
f ☐ The amount of money you pay for something.
g ☐ The activity of persuading people to buy something.
h ☐ Products which are not goods.

2 Complete the sentences with words from the text.

1 The interaction of supply and _____ determines what is produced and the quantity.
2 Customers prefer buying products with a low _____.
3 FIAT is an Italian car _____.
4 Banking is a type of _____.
5 _____ is when sellers try to be more successful than others in a market.
6 Every company wants to have a _____ from its sales.

3 Read the text and answer the questions.

1 Who is a seller and who is a buyer?
2 What is the difference between goods and services?
3 What is the difference between supply and demand?
4 Why is price an important factor in a market?
5 Do you agree that market demand influences what a producer puts in the market? Why?

4 Look at these two lists of similar words. Can you find any of them in the text?

to sell	to produce
seller	producer
sales	product
sales manager	production manager
sales department	production department

5 Are these goods or services? Label the pictures.

1 _____

2 _____

3 _____

4 _____

5 _____

6 _____

7 _____

8 _____

9 _____

10 _____

6 Now write 5 examples of goods and 5 examples of services typical of your country.

Goods
1 _____
2 _____
3 _____
4 _____
5 _____

Services
1 _____
2 _____
3 _____
4 _____
5 _____

7 Read the interview with Paul Laxer, an MP3 player manufacturer. Complete the dialogue with these questions.

> Does your company invest much in advertising
> ~~What exactly do you produce~~
> Do you mean that you beat the competition with low prices
> Is there much demand in the market for this type of product
> can we say that you're not worried about sales
> isn't there strong competition from mobile phones or smartphones

Interviewer: So, Mr Laxer. Tell us something about your company. (1) *What exactly do you produce*?

Mr Laxer: Well, we make MP3 players. We specialise in small, light, coloured, and of course, highly-technological MP3 players.

Interviewer: (2) _____ ?

Mr Laxer: Absolutely. At the beginning this product was just for young people. But now it's become very popular with older people as well. Today everybody listens to music anytime, anywhere.

Interviewer: I agree with you but (3) _____ _____ ?
I mean, there are so many mobile phones with this function.

Mr Laxer: It's true but still, our MP3 players have a good market. They have an unbeatable price compared to other similar articles and of course they're cheaper than good mobile phones.

Interviewer: (4) _____ ?

Mr Laxer: Yes, low prices combined with excellent quality, I would say.

Interviewer: (5) _____ ?

Mr Laxer: Not much. You see, our product has been on the market for a long time and has always been popular. So it's well-known and doesn't need too much advertising.

Interviewer: So, (6) _____ ?

Mr Laxer: Fortunately no, we aren't at the moment. But, you know, customers' needs may change at any time. We'll be ready when it happens.

8 **Read the text below and then match the beginnings and the ends of sentences 1 to 3.**

Never think that the world of business or of economy is far from you just because you are a teenager!
You are a consumer of goods and services which means that you play the rules of the market.
Like a lot of teenagers, you probably receive pocket money from your parents. Are there times when you can't do something with your pocket money because you don't have enough? Have you ever thought what this means in terms of economics? Let's look at an example.
Last Monday you received €20.00 as pocket money. On Friday afternoon you talk to your friends and discuss going to the cinema tonight and going to the disco together tomorrow night. You want to do both. Unfortunately you've already spent €9.00 and you don't want to ask your parents to give you your pocket money for next week in advance because this means that you won't receive any money next week. So you decide that you'll go to the cinema tonight (you have enough money for that) and you won't go to the disco. What does this means in terms of economy?

1 For you, as a customer, it means that
2 For the disco's owner, it means that

3 For the cinema's owner, it means

A he has earned more money.
B your choice is influenced by the costs of the two things you want to do.
C he has lost a customer.

Globalisation

Today we talk about the global market.
This means that the whole world has become a single marketplace and is not formed by different national markets. In other words, we are in an international market where companies have more opportunities to sell their products in any country in the world and customers have more opportunities to buy products from all over the world. In international economy this is called globalisation: the process by which companies operate in a lot of different countries all around the world.
What has facilitated this process of buying

and selling in the world market? One of the most important factors is that, over the past 20 years, there have been developments in new technology and in communication systems: thanks to the use of the Internet, email, mobile phones and video conferencing, companies can communicate 24 hours a day, 7 days a week. Also, improvements in transport and the reduction in restrictions to commerce (taxes on imports, for example) have given companies more opportunities in foreign markets and have contributed to free trade.

9 **Read the text about globalisation and decide if these statements are true (T) or false (F). Correct the false statements.**

1 Globalisation can be defined as the activity of buying and selling goods and services in all the countries in the world.   *T*
2 Globalisation started in 1920.   ____
3 Today people can communicate at any time on any day.   ____
4 Taxes on imports is an example of free trade.   ____
5 Today it is easier to transport goods from one country to another.   ____

10 🎧 1 **Globalisation is a very controversial problem. Read the list below. Then, listen to two experts talking about it and tick the advantages and disadvantages of globalisation they mention.**

Advantages	Disadvantages
1 Poor countries can develop economically. 2 Poor countries can improve their standard of living. 3 Globalisation is a force for democratic freedom. 4 Companies can sell more goods and make more money. 5 Globalisation creates more jobs. 6 There is more circulation of money. 7 Because of strong competition, prices are lower. 8 Thanks to globalisation, we know other cultures better.	1 Only multinationals, like Coca Cola or Nike, get the benefits. 2 Rich countries become richer at the expense of poor countries. 3 Globalisation destroys the environment in poor countries. 4 People who work for big multinationals are not well-paid. 5 Multinationals invest in poor countries so there are fewer jobs in rich countries. 6 Multinationals control the economy of poor countries. 7 Local cultures and traditions are not respected. 8 Workers in poor countries are exploited.

11 Writing **What's your opinion of globalisation? Write a text about it using the information from the text and from the two boxes in exercise 10. Follow these guidelines and use linkers and expressions from the box.**

Say what it is and how it has developed.
Say if you are in favour or against it and explain why.

first	then	also	finally
I think that		in my opinion	

MY GLOSSARY

advertising /ˈædvətaɪzɪŋ/ _____
amount /əˈmaʊnt/ _____
to beat /tə biːt/ _____
competition /kɒmpəˈtɪʃn/ _____
competitor /kəmˈpetɪtə(r)/ _____
consumer /kənˈsjuːmə(r)/ _____
customer /kɒsˈtjuːmə(r)/ _____
to demand /tə dɪˈmɑːnd/ _____
development /dɪˈveləpmənt/ _____

free trade /friː treɪd/ _____
goods /ɡʊdz/ _____
improvement /ɪmˈpruːvmənt/ _____
law of supply and demand /lɔː əv səˈplaɪ ən dɪˈmɑːnd/ _
manufacturer /mænjʊˈfæktʃrə(r)/ _____
profit /ˈprɒfɪt/ _____
to provide /tə prəˈvaɪd/ _____
restriction /rɪˈstrɪkʃn/ _____

3 Applying for a Job

When you finish high school or university, you will look for a job. The first step will be contacting the company you want to work for. How? With a job application which is a proposal to work for them.

1 The application process involves different steps. How do you think this process works? Put the steps in the correct order.

- ☐ The company reads your application, thinks you could be the right person and contacts you for an interview.
- ☐ You accept and start working for them.
- ☐ They contact you and offer you the job.
- ☐ You go to the interview.
- ☐ You send your application.
- ☑ You read an advertisement in which a company looks for a computer programmer.
- ☐ Your interview is successful.

We can say that the three main steps in the application process are:
1 Advertisement
2 Application
3 Interview
Let's look at them in detail.

First step: The advertisement

Job advertisements can be found on the Internet, on special sites or on company sites, but also in newspapers and magazines.

2 Read these two advertisements and answer the questions.

1

JOB: bank **cashier**
COMPANY: Walkers Bank
LOCATION: Boston
TERMS: **Permanent** / Full-time
DUTIES: customer service and administrative duties
EDUCATION: high school diploma
SKILLS: good **knowledge** of banking computer systems

<u>Click here to apply</u> or send an email plus CV to Staff Manager, <u>walkersbank@wb.org</u>

2

Experienced café **staff** needed to work at Party Café in Manchester.

You will be required to work from the end of November till the 23rd December.
There are various **shifts** and times **available**. Many of the shifts are in the evening allowing you to work around your studies or another job.

Part time **vacancies** available.

Email your application and CV to <u>jobs@cafebar.uk</u>

1 Which job is better for a student?
2 Which job is full-time only?
3 Which job is not permanent? When are you required to work?
4 Which job does not require a school diploma?
5 How can you apply for both of them?

Second step: The application

After reading a job advertisement, if you are interested in the job, you send your application, usually by email. Your application must include a CV (Curriculum Vitae). This a document with information about you and your work history. A CV must be clear and easy to read, so it must be organised into sections.

3 Look at this information from a CV and put it in the appropriate sections.

- Excellent English both written and spoken
- Email: c.parker@topmail.com
- 2008-2010: accountant at French Foods, 11 Avenue St Antoine, Nantes
- M. Gaston Artois, Directeur Général at French Foods
- 2007: High school diploma in accountancy from Lycée Saint-Louis, Tours

Section	Information
Personal information	
Work experience	
Education	
Skills	
References	

4 Two people have decided to apply for the post of bank cashier from the first advertisement on page 10. Read these two applications and match the descriptions in the box to the paragraphs.

attachments   education   work experience   opening (source of information + type of job)
references   skills   closing   salutation (opening greeting)   hope for interview

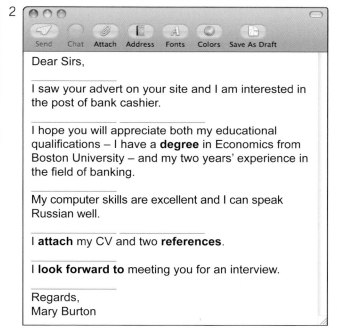

1

Dear Staff Manager,

I am writing to **apply** for the post of bank cashier advertised on your site.

As you can see from my CV, I got a high school diploma in 2009. Since then I have been working as a bank cashier for a major bank here in Boston where I **deal with** customers' **accounts** and sell financial products.

I hope you will contact me for an interview.

Best regards,
Paul Ascott

2

Dear Sirs,

I saw your advert on your site and I am interested in the post of bank cashier.

I hope you will appreciate both my educational qualifications – I have a **degree** in Economics from Boston University – and my two years' experience in the field of banking.

My computer skills are excellent and I can speak Russian well.

I **attach** my CV and two **references**.

I **look forward to** meeting you for an interview.

Regards,
Mary Burton

5 Complete the sentences with words from the box.

apply   application   deal with   attach   look forward to   interview   advertisement   duties   skills   knowledge

1 I _____ copies of my diplomas.
2 I have good _____ of French and Italian.
3 My _____ include organising meetings and events and advertising.
4 I would like to _____ for the post of computer programmer.
5 I saw your _____ in The Daily Telegraph and I am applying for the post of secretary.
6 I _____ your reply.
7 I am available for an _____ at any time.
8 In my present job, I _____ accounts.
9 Excellent computer _____ are required.
10 Please send your _____ to this email address.

6 These are the CVs that Paul Ascott and Mary Burton have attached to their applications. Read them and tick the table appropriately.

1

PERSONAL DETAILS
NAME: Paul Ascott
DATE OF BIRTH: 3/11/1991
ADDRESS: 15 Park Avenue, Boston
PHONE NO. 359 992177
EMAIL: paul.ascott@gmail.com

EDUCATION
2004-2009 High School Diploma –
High School West, Boston

PROFESSIONAL EXPERIENCE
2009 – present Atlantic Bank,
163 High Street, Boston – bank cashier
Duties: dealing with customers' accounts,
selling financial products

SKILLS
good knowledge of standard office
software

2

PERSONAL INFORMATION
Ms Mary Burton
Born in Boston on 15th June 1986
Married
35 San Diego Rd – Boston
(617) 466 2481
mburton@hotmail.com

EDUCATION
High School: 2000 – 2005 Parker High School, Boston
University: 2005 – 2009 Degree in Economics, Boston University

EMPLOYMENT
2009 – 2011 investment consultant at DT Bank – I assist customers
             in investments

SKILLS
Languages: Good Russian both written and spoken
Computer: Certificate in Microsoft Office

REFERENCES   George Brown   Gordon O'Neal
              Teacher of Economics   Manager
              Boston University   DT Bank State Street
              (617) 455 6002   (617) 430 8832
              gbrown@bu.com   gordononeal@dtbank.com

Who:	Paul Ascott	Mary Burton
has a degree?		
is still working?		
does not provide any references?		
can speak a foreign language?		
is married?		
has experience as a bank cashier?		
can use a computer?		
lives in Boston?		

7 Writing Now, you have decided to apply for the same post of bank cashier. Write your application email and CV using the information below. Use the layout and and vocabulary from the emails and CVs above to help.

- you have read the advertisement on the Internet
- you are 25, from Boston
- you have a high school diploma
- after school you worked for 3 years as a representative for a videogame company, then for 2 years as a bank clerk with administrative duties for a bank in Boston
- you have excellent computer knowledge
- you attach 1 reference

Third step: The interview

If your application is successful, the company contacts you for an interview before deciding whether to give you the job.

8 🎧 2 **This is a list of typical questions and answers during a job interview. First match these titles to the questions. Then match questions and answers. There may be more than one answer for each question.**

> Skills   Work experience
> Education   Interest in the job

Questions
1 What are your qualifications? *Education   e, f*
2 What school did you attend? _____
3 Tell me about your experience. _____
4 What work experience have you got?
_____
5 What are your duties? _____
6 What experience have you got in this field?
_____
7 Do you speak any foreign languages?
_____
8 What are your computer skills and what programs can you use? _____
9 Why do you want this job? _____
10 What interests you about this job? _____

Answers
a I am familiar with all the main computer programs.
b I have a good knowledge of computers.
c I think this job will improve my skills.
d I want to get experience in this field.
e I have a diploma in *accountancy* (and a degree in *Economics*).
f I went to *ITC Pascoli* in *Milan* and got my diploma *3 years ago*.
g I worked for an *import-export* company called *BC Ltd.* from *2008* to *2010*.
h I have several years of *office* experience.
i I am responsible for/My duties are *entering data into the computer* and *preparing statistical reports*.
j Yes, I can speak *English* fluently.

9 🎧 3 **Listen to Michael Green's interview for a job as an office clerk and decide if the statements are True (T) or False (F). Correct the false statements.**

1 Michael is 32.
2 He finished school 2 months ago.
3 He was a shop assistant in a sports store.
4 He has been working as a clerk since he stopped working for SportCentre.
5 He wants to leave his job because he wants to improve his office skills.
6 In his present job he does not use a computer.
7 He has no experience of office work.
8 He is good with computers.
9 He can't speak Italian.
10 He will be contacted in a couple of months.

10 **Now imagine you have applied for a job as a shop assistant in a music shop in London. Complete your interview with the missing words and phrases.**

Interviewer: Good morning and welcome.
You: (1) _____
I: I'd like to ask you a few questions. Let's start with education. What (2) _____ qualifications?
You: I (3) _____.
I: Fine. And (4) _____ in this field?
You: I (5) _____
I: Can you tell me about your computer (6) _____?
You: (7) _____.
I: That's great. Now, you can speak good English, but can you speak any other (8) _____?
You: (9) I _____.
I: I see. Now, one last question. Why (10) _____?
You: (11) _____.
I: OK. That's all for now. Thank you for coming. We'll contact you soon.
You: Thank you very much.

MY GLOSSARY

account /əˈkaʊnt/ _____
advertisement /ədˈvɜːtɪsmənt/ _____
to apply /tuː əˈplaɪ/ _____
to attach /tuː əˈtætʃ/ _____
available /əˈveɪləbl/ _____
cashier /kæˈʃɪə(r)/ _____
to deal with /tə diəl wɪð/ _____
degree /dɪˈgriː/ _____
duty /ˈdjuːti/ _____
education /edjʊˈkeɪʃn/ _____

interview /ˈɪntəvjuː/ _____
job application /dʒɒb æplɪˈkeɪʃn/ _____
knowledge /ˈn lɪdʒ/ _____
to look forward to /tə lʊk ˈfɔːwəd tə/ _____
permanent /ˈpɜːmənənt/ _____
reference /ˈrefrəns/ _____
shift /ʃɪft/ _____
skill /skɪl/ _____
staff /stɑːf/ _____
vacancy /ˈveɪkənsi/ _____

Using Business English does not only involve reading or writing emails, documents, or contracts but also speaking about business matters with other people.

Phone calls

When you work in a company, a lot of your work is done over the telephone, so being able to speak over the phone is a fundamental skill in business.

1 **Look at this list of typical sentences used when speaking on the phone and fill in the gaps with sentences from the box.**

> Right. I'll give him your message   I'm sorry but the line is busy.   Thank you. Goodbye.
> Can I speak to Jack Barnes, please?   Would you like to leave a message?   Yes, please. I'll hold.

Receiver

Brown Ltd, good morning. Can I help you?

Just a moment. I'll put you through.

I'm sorry but Mr Parker is not in the office.

(2) _____

(3) _____

Would you like to hold?

(5) _____

Right. I'll get him to call you back.

All right. I'll tell him that you called.

Thank you for calling. Goodbye.

Caller

Good morning. This is Ted Lee from Kelly & Sons.

(1) _____

Yes, please. Can you ask him to call me back, please?

(4) _____

It's OK, thanks. I'll call back later.

(6) _____

2 🎧 4 **Listen to a phone call and complete it with the missing words and phrases.**

Operator: (1) _____. Delta Limited. Can I help you?

Karen Mills: Ah, yes, good morning. (2) _____ Karen Mills from Jenkins Marketing. (3) _____ Jan Dixon, please?

Operator: Good morning Mrs Mills. (4) _____. I'll put you through... I'm sorry, Mrs Mills, but (5) _____. Would you like to hold or (6) _____?

Karen Mills: I'll leave a message. Can you ask him to (7) _____, please? I'd like to ask him a few questions about his last order.

Operator: No problem. I'll (8) _____ to call you back as soon as he's free. Thanks (9) _____. Goodbye.

Karen Mills: Thank you. (10) _____.

3 Tom White works for a company called Scott Bikes. He calls one of his customers, Action Sports, and asks to speak to Alice Ellis. The operator connects him but then says that the line is engaged. He says he'll call back later. Complete the dialogue.

Operator: Good morning. (1) _____?
Tom White: Good morning (2) _____.
Operator: Just (3) _____. I'll (4) _____
                     _____ ... I'm sorry (5) _____. Would you like
                     (6) _____?
Tom White: It's (7) _____.
Operator: OK, Mr White. I'll tell Mrs Ellis that (8) _____.
Tom White: Thanks.
Operator: Thank you for (9) _____.
Tom White: (10) _____.

Fixing appointments

One of the reasons people speak over the phone is to fix appointments and organise meetings.

4 Can you complete the translations of these typical questions and answers? When you have finished, check the translations with your partner.

> A: Can we / I'd like to fix an appointment (?)
>   (1) _____
> B: Yes, certainly. Let me get my diary.
>   (2) _____

B: Is Tuesday at 10 OK for you?
     (3) _____
A: I'm afraid I'm busy. Shall we meet on / What about Tuesday afternoon, instead?
     (4) _____
B: Yes, that's fine. Shall we make it 3 o'clock?
     (5) _____
A: OK. I'll see you on Tuesday at 3 in your office, then.
     (6) _____

B: When would be convenient for you?
     (7) _____
A: I'm free on Friday morning.
     (8) _____
B: OK. What time shall we meet?
     (9) _____
A: Shall we say at 10? / Would 10 be OK for you?
     (10) _____
B: That's fine. See you on Friday at 10 in your office, then.
     (11) _____

4

5 🎧 5 **Listen to a phone call and complete the memo.**

> ARTTOUCH LTD.
>
> To: (1) _____
> Name of caller: (2) _____
> Company: (3) _____
> Phone number: (4) _____
> Message: (5) _____

6 🎧 6 **Listen to a phone call between Brett Collins and Sarah Young and choose the correct alternative.**

1 Brett Collins...
  a wants to speak to Sarah Young.
  b receives a phone calls from Sarah Young.
2 a Brett
  b Sarah   wants to fix an appointment.
3 Brett is...
  a free on Monday and Wednesday afternoon.
  b busy
4 They decide to meet on...
  a Monday.
  b Wednesday.
5 They will meet at...
  a 5.
  b 3.

7 Writing **Write the dialogue following the instructions.**

Operator:	*(Answer the phone. The name of your company is Martins Electronics.)*
Henry Palmer:	*(Greet. Say your name. You work for Olsen Ltd. You want to speak to Matt Russell.)*
Operator:	*(Ask him to hold. Put Matt Russell through.)*
Henry Palmer:	*(Thank him.)*
Matt Russell:	*(Greet Mr Palmer. Ask him how he is.)*
Henry Palmer:	*(You are fine, now ask him.)*
Matt Russell:	*(You are fine. Ask him what you can do for him.)*
Henry Palmer:	*(You want to fix an appointment for the next month. Suggest Wednesday 18th.)*
Matt Russell:	*(You are busy. Suggest Friday 20th.)*
Henry Palmer:	*(Accept. Ask him morning or afternoon.)*
Matt Russell:	*(Suggest 9 in the morning in your office.)*
Henry Palmer:	*(You have another appointment at 9. Suggest 11.)*
Matt Russell:	*(Accept. Repeat the details of the appointment.)*
Henry Palmer:	*(Confirm. Thank. Say goodbye.)*
Matt Russell:	*(Thank. Say goodbye.)*

Discussing

Working in a company also means discussing issues, comparing different opinions and reaching an agreement.

Asking for opinions	Expressing opinions	Agreeing and disagreeing
What do you think about (that)? What's your opinion of (that)?	I think that... I'm sure that...	I agree with you. I think you're right. I don't know. / I'm not sure about that. I don't think you're right. I'm sorry but I don't agree. I disagree (completely).

8 Read the dialogue and complete the table. Tick (✓) the things they like and put a cross (✗) for the things they don't like.

Paul: So, let's talk about these proposals for our new advertising campaign. What do you think about it, Liz?

Liz: I think the TV ad is really great but the photos used for the advertisement on our website are terrible.

Jason: I agree with you. I mean, about the photos, I don't like them either. But I'm not sure the TV ad is good. I think it's too long.

Paul: Yes, I think you're right. The TV ad should be shorter. But I think that the online advertisement is fantastic – photos included. Anyway, what's your opinion of the gadgets? I think they're 'special'. Do you agree?

Jason: Absolutely. I agree completely.

Liz: Well, I'm sorry but I don't agree. We should find something better.

	Paul	Liz	Jason
TV ad			
website advert			
gadgets			

9 Read the dialogue and put the sentences in the correct order.

☐1 Ann: As you know, a new Swedish customer, FCF Corporation, has just contacted us for a very large order of our crash helmets. We have to discuss what terms to give him. I mean price, discount and payment terms. Let's start with price. What do you think?

☐ Alex: I agree with you. So let's tell him that we can't and ask him to pay when he receives the goods.

☐ Ann: Yes, Alex, I think you're right. It's a good price. But his order is very large, so I think we should give him a good discount, let's say 15%.

☐ Ann: OK, 10% then. Now, he asks to pay after 30 days. I'm sure that we've never given these terms to any of our customers for their first order.

☐ Alex: I don't agree. 15% is too high. Let's make it 10%.

☐ Ann: All right. I agree. I'll send him an email immediately.

☐ Alex: Well, I don't think we should change our catalogue price which is very competitive.

MY GLOSSARY

advertising campaign /ˈædvətaɪzɪŋ kæmˈpeɪn/ _____

crash helmet /kræʃ ˈhelmɪt/ _____

discount /ˈdɪskaʊnt/ _____

17

5 | Writing Business Emails

The most common form of written communication in business is email (*electronic mail*). Therefore, the ability to use email well is very important for anybody working in a company.
If you already use emails to communicate with friends, you know how many advantages it has.

1 **This is a list of some advantages of communicating by email. Match the beginnings of the sentences to the endings.**

1 Sending emails is fast and
2 You can send emails any time and
3 You can attach files
4 You can send emails wherever you are
5 You can send the same email to
6 Using emails saves the time of printing, copying and
7 You can store your emails and find them quickly when

A (no matter how 'heavy' they are).
B a large number of people.
C you need them.
D distributing information to many people.
E simple.
F (but you must have a computer or a smart phone).
G anywhere.

2 **Why do business people use emails? Read this interview with a businessman and find 4 reasons he gives for using email.**

Interviewer: So, Mr Randall, let's talk about your relationship with your computer. Could we say that you can't live without it?
Tim Randall: Absolutely! I don't do anything and I don't go anywhere without it. I travel a lot and I hate talking over the phone. So everything related to my work I do with my computer.
Interviewer: But what do you do with your computer most of all?
Tim Randall: I read and send emails. I can send and read hundreds of emails every day.
Interviewer: Hundreds? That's unbelievable.
Tim Randall: It's not if you think of how many reasons you have to send or read emails.
Interviewer: Tell me about it.
Tim Randall: Well, first of all I send information to customers, to colleagues. And of course I receive information from them. Then, giving instructions. For example to people who work for me.
Interviewer: And do you ever use emails for appointments or do you use the telephone for that?
Tim Randall: Sure. I use email to fix or change appointments. And I also use emails when I need to send documents, like offers or reports.

He uses email:
1 to _____ and _____
2 to _____
3 to _____ or _____
4 to _____

Like any document, an email has a standard format: it is organised in different parts.

3 **Look at this email and label the parts correctly.**

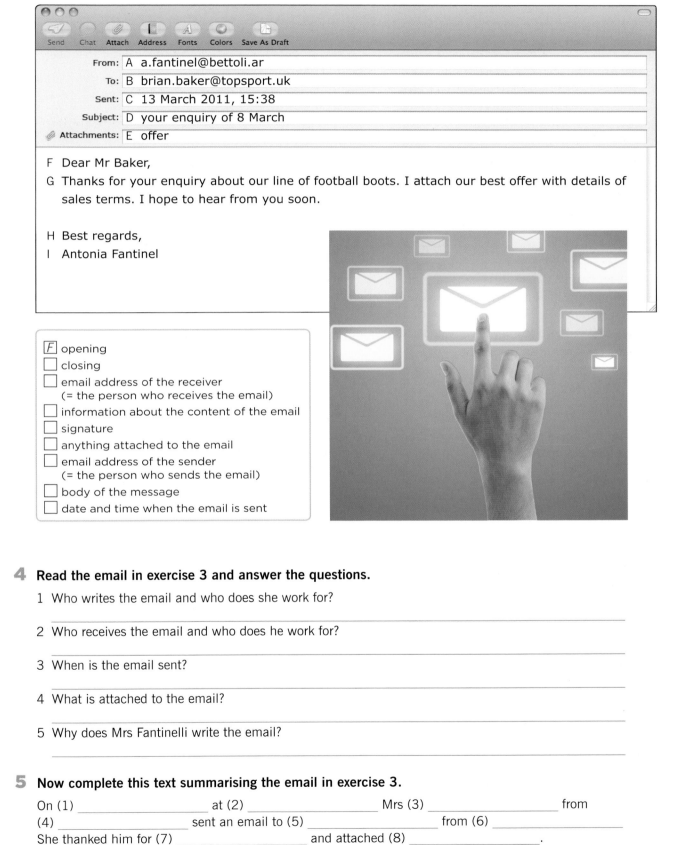

From:	A	a.fantinel@bettoli.ar
To:	B	brian.baker@topsport.uk
Sent:	C	13 March 2011, 15:38
Subject:	D	your enquiry of 8 March
Attachments:	E	offer

F Dear Mr Baker,

G Thanks for your enquiry about our line of football boots. I attach our best offer with details of sales terms. I hope to hear from you soon.

H Best regards,

I Antonia Fantinel

- [F] opening
- [ ] closing
- [ ] email address of the receiver (= the person who receives the email)
- [ ] information about the content of the email
- [ ] signature
- [ ] anything attached to the email
- [ ] email address of the sender (= the person who sends the email)
- [ ] body of the message
- [ ] date and time when the email is sent

4 **Read the email in exercise 3 and answer the questions.**

1 Who writes the email and who does she work for?

_____

2 Who receives the email and who does he work for?

_____

3 When is the email sent?

_____

4 What is attached to the email?

_____

5 Why does Mrs Fantinelli write the email?

_____

5 **Now complete this text summarising the email in exercise 3.**

On (1) _____ at (2) _____ Mrs (3) _____ from
(4) _____ sent an email to (5) _____ from (6) _____
She thanked him for (7) _____ and attached (8) _____ .

5

When you write an email you must follow some rules about language, style and structure.
These questions can help you write the perfect email.

1   Is the message short and clear?
2   Are grammar and spelling correct?
3   Are the attachments mentioned in the message attached?
4   Are paragraphs separated by a line space?
5   Is the subject included and is it clear?
6   Does the body contains all standard parts (opening, body, closing and signature)?

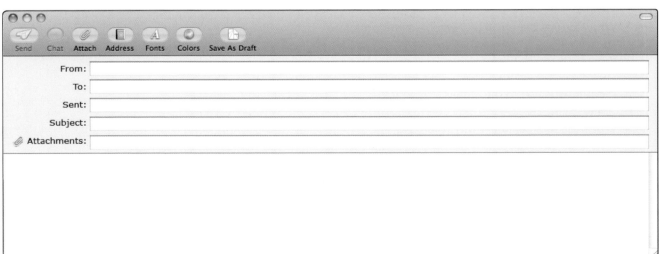

Send   Chat   Attach   Address   Fonts   Colors   Save As Draft

From: tina.richardson@fandsons.uk
To: j.owens@citybank.com
Sent: 8 August 2011, 08:12
Subject:
Attachments:

Dear Mrs Owens,

Following our telepone conversation, I would like to fix an appointment for next 20 august at 10, if that is OK for you.

I have attach the documents we will discuss together.

Please confirm our appointment.

Best regards,

Tina richardson

6   **Read the email above, ask the questions 1 to 6 in the box and take notes of your answers to decide if it is a 'perfect' email or not.**

1 _____
2 _____
3 _____
4 _____
5 _____
6 _____

7   Writing **Now rewrite the email correctly.**

Send   Chat   Attach   Address   Fonts   Colors   Save As Draft

From:
To:
Sent:
Subject:
Attachments:

8 🎧 7 **Listen to a businesswoman dictating an email to her secretary and complete the email.**

From: clare.taylor@globalnet.com
To: (1) _____
Sent: 10 July 2011, 11:45
Subject: (2) _____
Attachments: (3) _____

Dear (4) _____,

Thanks for (5) _____ of
(6) _____.
Unfortunately I have to (7) _____ of
2 August as I have another
(8) _____. Can we meet on 3 August
at (9) _____?

I look forward to your reply.
Best regards,
Clare (10) _____

9 Writing **Read the situation and complete the email.**

On 5ᵗʰ November 2011, at 2.32 in the afternoon, Carmen Lopez (c.lopez@garcia.com) sends an email to one of her customers, Dario Randi (dario.randi@marcolongo.it) to thank him for his order of 27ᵗʰ October. She attaches the details of their sales terms and asks for confirmation before sending the material.

From:
To:
Sent:
Subject:
Attachments:

MY GLOSSARY

to attach /tuː əˈtætʃ/ _____
attachment /əˈtætʃmənt/ _____
content /ˈkɒntent/ _____
detail /ˈdiːteɪl/ _____
enquiry /ɪnˈkwaɪəri/ _____

sales terms /seɪls tɜːmz/ _____
signature /ˈsɪɡnətʃə(r)/ _____
to store /tə stɔː(r)/ _____
subject /ˈsʌbdʒəkt/ _____

If an entrepreneur wants to start a business, he has a lot of important decisions to take – for example, what to produce, where to get the capital from and what type of company to set up. This one is a crucial point because there are different opportunities, but one of the most popular today is a franchise like McDonald's, Benetton or H&M.

1 Think of a franchise restaurant or store you know. What are its characteristics? Circle Yes or No in the table and then correct.

They sell the same products/ goods.	Yes No	
You can't find them in different towns and countries.	Yes No	
Prices are similar in different countries.	Yes No	
They have the same logo.	Yes No	
They never have the same shop furniture.	Yes No	
They use different types of advertising.	Yes No	

But what exactly is franchise? Read the definition.
A franchise is a contract between two parties – the franchisor and the franchisee.
The franchisee is a small business owner who sells goods or services produced by a large company, called the franchisor, in exchange for some payment (a fee plus a percentage of the profit).

2 Who do these statements refer to? Write Franchisor or Franchisee.

1 provides the logo _____
2 sells a well-known product _____
3 invests in research and promotion _____
4 has a network of outlets in different geographical areas _____
5 uses a famous trademark _____
6 is obliged to buy exclusively from one company _____
7 has the exclusive right to sell those goods in his geographical area _____

3 Look at the words A and B and choose the best alternative to complete the sentences.

1 The new Coca Cola _____ campaign is fantastic.   A company   B advertising
2 Mr Johnson is the _____ of this restaurant.   A owner   B trademark
3 Please send the _____ by train.   A profit   B goods
4 We want to _____ a new company.   A set up   B provide
5 IKEA has a lot of _____ in Europe.   A outlets   B business
6 I hope I become a successful _____.   A fee   B entrepreneur

Another form of business organisation is an unlimited partnership. It is formed by two or more owners (called partners) who share the management and financial responsibility for the business. This means that they take decisions together, share profits but are also responsible for the company's debts. What does that mean? It means that if the company goes bankrupt, they have to pay for the debts with their personal possessions.

4 **Read the text above about unlimited partnership and answer the questions.**

1 Who forms an unlimited partnership?

_____

2 What are the members of an unlimited partnership called?

_____

3 What are the advantages of this type of business organisation?

_____

4 What is the disadvantage?

_____

5 **Match the words in the left hand column with their definitions in the right hand column.**

1 profit
2 trademark
3 to go bankrupt
4 outlet
5 debts

a ☐ shop
b ☐ sum of money that you have to pay
c ☐ the money that remains after paying costs
d ☐ name of a product than can't be used by any other company
e ☐ to be unable to pay your debts

6 🎧 8 **Listen to two entrepreneurs talking about their businesses and complete the table.**

Name of company		
When it was set up		
Type of business		
Advantages		
Disadvantages		

7 **Go back to all the information about franchises and unlimited partnerships and prepare a spoken presentation following these guidelines:**

- name and definition of the people involved
- their duties/responsibilities
- the reason(s) why you think you would(n't) like to set one up

These sentences may help you:

The people involved in _____ are called _____.
These are their/his responsibilities/duties: _____.
I would(n't) like to set up a _____ because _____.

6

Company organisation

There are many things to be done in a company, for example: buy materials, produce the goods, contact and sell to clients, administer the company's finances. This is why there are different departments responsible for the various tasks.

8 **These are some basic departments. Can you choose what each of the departments does from the box below?**

> buys all materials necessary for production   organises advertising and product promotion
> looks after the company staff   deals with the company's financial matters
> is responsible for selling what the company produces   makes the products

1 production department _____
2 sales department _____
3 finance department _____
4 human resources department _____
5 marketing department _____
6 purchasing department _____

The structure or organisation of a company can be graphically shown in an organigram, that is a diagram representing all departments. On top of this chart there is a Board of Directors, a group of people who control the company.

9 🎧 9 **This is the organigram of an English company called F&M Ltd. Listen to some managers who work there and complete the chart with their names in the correct department.**

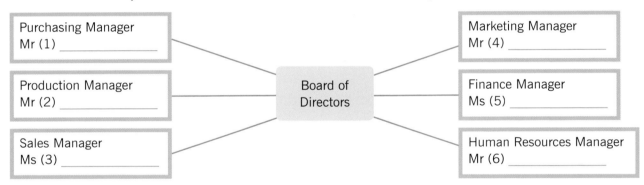

Purchasing Manager Mr (1) _____		Marketing Manager Mr (4) _____
Production Manager Mr (2) _____	Board of Directors	Finance Manager Ms (5) _____
Sales Manager Ms (3) _____		Human Resources Manager Mr (6) _____

10 **Read the story of Richard Turner and do the exercises which follow.**

When he was 21, Richard Turner started working as an <u>accountant</u> for a mobile phone company. 'I sat at my PC in the office and checked the <u>invoices</u> and payments all day, every day. I didn't like my job – it was so boring and repetitive. But I was ambitious: I wanted to gain experience in the accounting field and maybe have my own business one day' he says. So, he stayed in the company for about 10 years with no hope of progressing in his career.

One day, he went to a party and met Brian Harris, an old schoolmate. Brian was an agent – he worked for a company called GameWorld Ltd which produced video games. They talked for a while and Richard told Brian that he wasn't happy with his job. His friend said that his company was looking for somebody to work in the Finance Department, so Richard <u>applied</u> for the post. He sent his CV and went for an <u>interview</u>.

In a couple of months he was an accountant at GameWorld Ltd. The atmosphere was completely different: it was a dynamic company where people could take the initiative and progress in their careers. Besides, in five years, the company grew considerably, controlling about 30% of the market in England.

Richard became the Finance Department manager two years ago. 'I still work on everything related to money, that is <u>expenditure</u> and costs.' he says. 'But the difference is that now I don't do it personally – I coordinate a team that checks invoices and payments like I used to do!'

11 Match the words to their definitions.

1 accountant   a ☐ a document showing how much you owe someone for goods or a service
2 invoice   b ☐ the total amount of money that people or organizations spend during a period of time
3 to apply   c ☐ a meeting in which someone asks you questions to see if you are suitable for a job
4 interview   d ☐ to make a formal request
5 expenditure   e ☐ someone whose job is to keep and check financial accounts

12 Choose the best title for each paragraph.

1 Richard's recent successful career   Paragraph _____
2 Richard's first job   Paragraph _____
3 His start at GameWorld Ltd.   Paragraph _____
4 A fantastic job opportunity   Paragraph _____

13 Decide if these statements are T (True) or F (False). Correct the false sentences.

1 Richard worked for his first company for about 10 years.
2 He didn't like his first job but he had no ambition.
3 He heard about the post in the Finance Department at GameWorld Ltd. from a newspaper.
4 The new company was better than the old one.
5 He became a manager as soon as he started working for GameWorld Ltd.

14 Writing Write a summary of the article including the information below (about 100 words).

- what his first job was, whether he liked it and why
- why he applied for the post at GameWorld Ltd.
- why he liked working there
- what career progression he had at GameWorld Ltd
- what his present responsibilities are

MY GLOSSARY

business /'bɪznəs/ _____
company /'kʌmpəni/ _____
debt /det/ _____
department /dɪ'paːtmənt/ _____
entrepreneur /ɒntrəprə'nɜː(r)/ _____
fee /fiː/ _____
to go bankrupt /tə gəʊ 'bæŋkrʌpt/ _____
human resources /'hjuːmən rɪ'zɔːsɪz/ _____
management /'mænɪdʒmənt/ _____

outlet /'aʊtlet/ _____
owner /'əʊnə(r)/ _____
profit /'prɒfɪt/ _____
purchasing /'pɜːtʃəsɪŋ/ _____
sales /seɪls/ _____
to set up /tə set ʌp/ _____
trademark /'treɪdmaːk/ _____
unlimited partnership /ʌn'lɪmɪtɪd 'paːtnəʃɪp/ _____

7 The Business Transaction

Business involves buying and selling goods or services. When a buyer buys from a seller (and a seller sells to a buyer), this is called a business transaction.

1 **There are different steps in a business transaction. Look at this flow chart showing the 4 basic steps and match them with the corresponding explanation.**

Enquiry

The seller confirms he has received the order and sends the goods to the buyer.

Reply to enquiry

The buyer needs a product. He contacts a seller and asks for information about, for example, type of product, costs, discounts, delivery time, payment terms, means of transport.

Order

If the terms received from the seller are satisfactory, the buyer sends an order. He specifies the article he wants to buy, its quantity and price, and all the terms: discount, payment, transport.

Reply to order

The seller receives the enquiry from the buyer and gives him the information requested.

2 🎧 10 **Listen to 8 sentences taken from 8 dialogues and write which steps of a business transactions they refer to.**

1 _____
2 _____
3 _____
4 _____

5 _____
6 _____
7 _____
8 _____

3 **You will see these words and expressions in the emails in exercise 4. Can you guess what they mean? Write the corresponding word in your language.**

1 item   a _____
2 discount   b _____
3 to deliver   c _____
4 hear from you   d _____
5 to look forward to   e _____
6 (best) regards   f _____
7 to attach   g _____
8 catalogue   h _____
9 receipt   i _____
10 dear   j _____

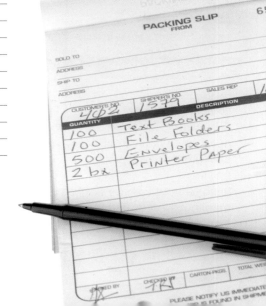

4 Read these 2 emails written by a buyer and seller and complete the table.

	The buyer	The seller
Product	He wants to know if _____	He replies that they do and _____
Discount	He asks what _____	He replies that _____
Delivery	He asks when _____	He replies that _____

5 After receiving the reply from Beston Sportstuff, Anthony Reynolds from Future Sport sends this order. Read it and find this information.

1 How many items he orders: _____

2 What type of articles he orders: _____

3 How much each item costs: _____

4 How much he will pay in total: _____

5 When he wants to receive the goods: _____

6 How he will pay: _____

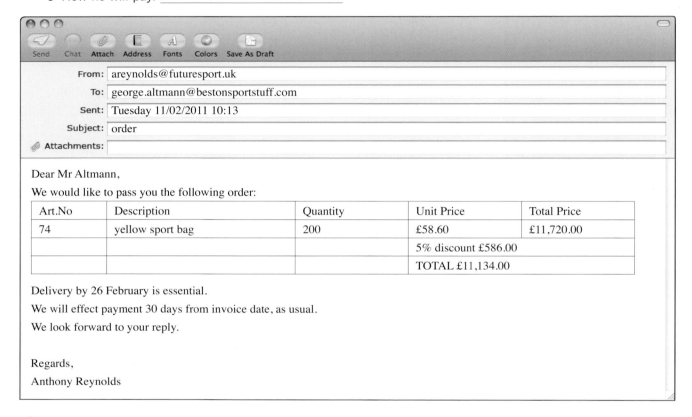

From: areynolds@futuresport.uk
To: george.altmann@bestonsportstuff.com
Sent: Tuesday 11/02/2011 10:13
Subject: order
Attachments:

Dear Mr Altmann,

We would like to pass you the following order:

Art.No	Description	Quantity	Unit Price	Total Price
74	yellow sport bag	200	£58.60	£11,720.00
			5% discount £586.00	
			TOTAL £11,134.00	

Delivery by 26 February is essential.

We will effect payment 30 days from invoice date, as usual.

We look forward to your reply.

Regards,

Anthony Reynolds

6 This is Beston Sportstuff's reply. Read it and circle Yes or No to these questions.

1 Does Mr Altmann confirm receipt of the order from Future Sport?   Yes / No

2 Will the goods be delivered when the client wants?   Yes / No

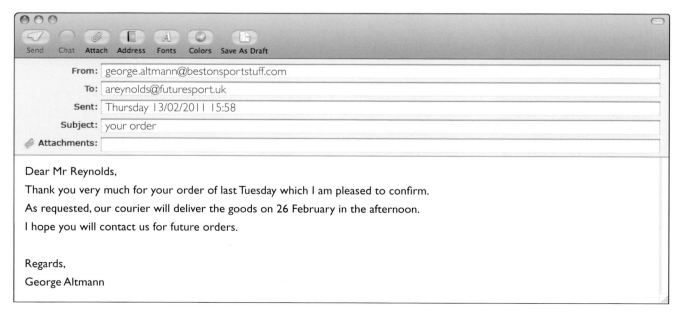

From: george.altmann@bestonsportstuff.com
To: areynolds@futuresport.uk
Sent: Thursday 13/02/2011 15:58
Subject: your order
Attachments:

Dear Mr Reynolds,

Thank you very much for your order of last Tuesday which I am pleased to confirm.

As requested, our courier will deliver the goods on 26 February in the afternoon.

I hope you will contact us for future orders.

Regards,

George Altmann

7 Complete these enquiry and reply emails using words and phrases from the emails in this unit.

The enquiry

> Send Chat Attach Address Fonts Colors Save As Draft
>
> (1) _____ Mrs Smart,
>
> I (2) _____ to ask if you can send us your best price for your mobile phone covers, art.no. AA64 of your catalogue.
> (3) _____ also let us know about possible discounts, delivery times and means of payment requested?
> We look (4) _____ .
>
> Best (5) _____ ,
> David Hobbs

The reply

> Send Chat Attach Address Fonts Colors Save As Draft
>
> Dear (6) _____ ,
>
> Many (7) _____ your enquiry about our mobile phone covers. I (8) _____ a copy of our catalogue with information about the article. For an order of about 100 items, we can (9) _____ 10% (10) _____ .
> We (11) _____ delivery
> (12) _____ 1 month from
> (13) _____ .
> We require (14) _____ 30 days from
> (15) _____ .
> We look (16) _____ your order.
>
> (17) _____ ,
> Margaret Smart

The order

8 🎧 11 **David Hobbs decides to send an order to Margaret Smart. Listen to him talking about the order with his secretary and complete the order form they will send to their supplier.**

> Order Form
> Contact: David Hobbs

Art.No	Colour	Quantity	Unit Price
____	____	____	____
____	____	____	____
____	____	____	____

> Delivery: _____
> Payment: _____

The reply to the order

9 Writing **Write the reply to David Hobbs' order from Margaret Smart following the guidelines below.**

- thank him for his order and confirm it
- say that delivery will be effected as requested
- say you hope he will contact you for future orders

* For orders in detail see Unit 10 Placing Orders

MY GLOSSARY

as requested /əz rɪˈkwestɪd/ _____
courier /ˈkʊriə(r)/ _____
delivery /dɪˈlɪvri/ _____
to effect /tuː ɪˈfekt/ _____

invoice /ˈɪnvɔɪs/ _____
means /miːnz/ _____
pleased /pliːzd/ _____
term /tɜːm/ _____

8 Trade Documentation

Any business transaction involves a number of documents. The most common are related to
■ the sale of goods
■ the transport of the goods
■ the payment of the goods

The document related to the sale of goods is called an invoice. It is a document issued by a seller to a buyer and it shows details of the goods sold (quantity, description, price), name and contact information of both the seller and the buyer, as well as payment terms. It must contain a number and a date.

The transport document depends on the means of transport used. In fact, goods can be transported by train, by lorry, by ship or by plane. This document is issued by the transport company which takes the goods and delivers them to the buyer. It contains the name and contact information of the seller, the buyer and the carrier, details of the goods (quantity, description and size) and all information about when and where the goods leave and arrive.

Payments involve banks that move money from the buyer's bank account to the seller's bank account. One of the most frequently used means is the bank transfer.
The choice of which payment terms to use in a business transaction depends on different factors. One factor is the relationship between the seller and the buyer because some means of payment can be safer for the seller: for example, payment in advance, which means that the buyer pays before receiving the goods. On the other hand, the means of payment that gives the maximum security to the buyer but represents the greatest risk to the seller is open account terms in which the buyer agrees to pay the seller's invoice at a future date, usually in 30 to 90 days. This means of payment is used only if the buyer is financially reliable and the seller trusts him.

1 Answer the questions.

1 What document refers to the sale of goods? _____
2 Who issues it? _____
3 How many means of transport can you think of? _____
4 Can you give a definition of carrier? _____
5 What does payment in advance consist of? _____
6 When does a buyer usually pay on open account terms? _____

2 Look at this table. Tick (✓) the documents where you can find these elements.

	Invoice	Transport document	Payment document
Buyer's name			
Seller's name			
Carrier's name			
Details of the goods			
Name of bank			

D&M Fashion is an English company that makes accessories. One of its customers, an Italian shop, has sent them an order. Let's look at the documents in the transaction.

The invoice

3 **Look at the invoice and answer the questions.**

D&M Fashion
www.dandm.com
15 Lockett Street
Manchester, M8 8EE
Tel.: 0161 8349652
Fax: 0161 8349655
info@dandm.com

Invoice no.: 45/A
Invoice date: 14 April 2011

Order no.: 66/11
Order date: 2 March 2011

Buyer: Nonsologioielli
             Via Oriani 35
             48121 Ravenna
             Italy

Quantity	Cat.No	Description	Unit Price	Total Price
40	A52	ear ring	£12.50	£500.00
50	A55	ear ring	£10.90	£545.00
35	G63	ring	£7.80	£273.00
65	H87	bracelet	£22.40	£1456.00
				Total: £2774.00

Payment Terms: bank transfer 30 days from invoice date

1   What's the exporter's name?
2   What's the importer's name?
3   Where are the two companies based?
4   When is the invoice issued?
5   When did the buyer send his order?
6   What are the invoice and the order numbers?
7   How many different types of articles does the buyer buy?
8   What is the most expensive article?
9   How does the buyer pay?
10 What is the total amount of the invoice?

4 **Complete this text summarising the invoice.**

This document is an (1) _____ sent by (2) _____ to one of its customers called (3) _____ .
The invoice is issued on (4) _____ 2011 and it refers to order no. (5) _____ of (6) _____ 2011. The Italian customer buys earrings, (7) _____ and (8) _____ for a total quantity of (9) _____ items and for a total amount of (10) £ _____ .

The transport document

Nonsologioielli needs the accessories urgently, so they require transport by air. The transport document used in transport by air is called an Air Waybill.

5 🎧 12 **Listen to Diana Downing, who works for the courier transporting the goods ordered by Nonsologioielli. She is writing the Air Waybill with a colleague. Complete it.**

	406 – 0000 0000
Consignor's name: (1) _____ 15 Lockett Street Manchester, M8 8EE	548 – 4310 – 9022 Air waybill issued by: UK World Courier 72 Maple Road Manchester M3 2BY
Consignee's name: Nonsologioielli Via Oriani 35 (2) _____ Ravenna Italy	
Airport of **departure**: (3) _____	Airport of destination: (4) _____
Flight no.: BA 399	Flight Date: (5) _____ 2011

No. of **packages** (6) _____	**Gross weight** (7) _____ ,80kg	Nature and Quantity of Goods *(including dimensions or volume)* 1 box 40cm x 30cm x 15cm

Signature of Issuing Carrier: *Diana Downing*	Date: (8) _____ /04/2011

N.O.3
ORIGINAL FOR
SHIPPER   **406 – 0000 0000**

6 **Read the Air Waybill and find this information.**

1 The number of the Air Waybill and date issued: _____
2 The name of the courier: _____
3 Where the goods leave from: _____
4 When the goods leave: _____
5 Where the goods arrive: _____
6 The number of boxes, their weight and dimensions: _____

The payment document

As we know from the invoice on page 31, Nonsologioielli has to pay by bank transfer 30 days from the date of the invoice.

7 Look at the bank transfer issued by their bank. What do you think IBAN and BIC stand for? Use some of the words in the box. Then check under the document.

> number   amount   international   customer   account   identification   identifier   nation   code   bank

IBAN: _____

BIC: _____

```
Deutsche Bank
C.so Cavour 58
8121 Ravenna
Italy
Customer's name: Nonsologioielli
IBAN IT57S0100503392000000218192
BIC: BDMRIT3GXXX

Amount to pay: £2774.00
Reference: Invoice No. 45/A of 14/04/2011

Beneficiary's name: D&M FASHION
Beneficiary's IBAN: GB15400515128834735678
Bank name: Allied Banks plc
BIC: ALBS8355XXX
```

IBAN = International Bank Account Number
BIC = Bank Identifier Code

8 Complete these sentences and describe the document.

1 This document is a

2 It is issued by

3 This bank transfer is ordered by

4 The bank transfer is for the amount of

5 This amount refers to

6 The bank that receives the amount is

7 The English bank transfers the amount to the account of

9 Insurance

What is insurance?

Insurance is the way in which people and businesses protect themselves against risks. Individuals and businesses want protection from the financial consequences of something unexpected or unpleasant happening. Insurance transfers the risk from them to someone else, the insurance company.

In the UK, some kinds of insurance are **compulsory** for individuals, like motor insurance for driving a car or buildings insurance if you have a mortgage on your home. Other kinds of insurance, such as protection against theft, accident or illness, are **optional**.

When a person or a business wishes to take out insurance, they can either contact an insurance company directly or they can use an **insurance broker**. This is an independent company or individual who advises on and then sells the best policy. The client then pays a fee, or premium, to the insurer which underwrites the policy, that is the insurance company which takes on the risk. The details of what is covered and in what circumstances are all set out in the insurance policy, which has to be renewed periodically, normally every year. If a policyholder makes a valid claim, the insurer will pay out the amount of compensation agreed. Insurance companies, like most other business, are profit-making organisations so they invest the premiums they receive and naturally hope that they do not have to pay out more in claims than they get back in premiums in a year.

1 Read the text and decide if these sentences are true (T) or false (F). If there is not enough information, choose 'doesn't say' (DS).

1 Insurance is a kind of financial protection for both individuals and businesses. _____
2 A driver must have motor insurance for his/her car. _____
3 A company is not obliged to have any kind of insurance. _____
4 Insurance brokers work for insurance companies. _____
5 Insurance premiums increase annually. _____
6 It is necessary to renew insurance policies. _____
7 Most insurance claims are for theft. _____
8 If an insurance company had to pay out a lot of claims, it could lose money. _____

2 Match each word with the correct definition.

1 premium   a ☐ the money awarded to a victim of loss/damage by an insurance company
2 policy   b ☐ a demand for money under the conditions of an insurance policy
3 policyholder   c ☐ the amount of money to be paid for an insurance contract
4 underwrite   d ☐ the person or company that issues the insurance contract
5 risk   e ☐ the person or company who offers advice and sells insurance company
6 insurer   f ☐ the insurance contract
7 broker   g ☐ a possibility of harm or damage, physical or financial
8 claim   h ☐ to sign and accept liability
9 compensation   i ☐ the person/business in whose name the insurance contract is held

Business insurance

As mentioned previously, there are two types of compulsory insurance for businesses in the UK:
- **Employers' liability insurance.** This insures all company employees against injury, disease or death as a result of their employment, workplace conditions or practices.
- **Motor insurance.** This is compulsory if the company owns and operates any kind of vehicle on public roads.

However, no modern business would operate solely with compulsory insurance. If something went wrong – a fire in a production plant, the theft of goods, injury to a customer – it would cost the company a great deal of money and it could even force them out of business. Therefore it is normal to take out insurance policies to cover further risks and liabilities. The different kinds of business insurance can be divided into three main areas:

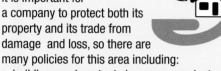

Protection against loss or damage

It is important for a company to protect both its property and its trade from damage and loss, so there are many policies for this area including:
- buildings and contents insurance against fire, lightning, explosion, floods, etc;
- cover against electrical and mechanical breakdown of machinery, including computers;
- contents insurance against theft, which can also include a money policy to cover cash, cheques, postage stamps and other negotiable documents;
- insurance of goods in transit;
- cover against business interruption and loss of income;
- trade credit cover, which may be particularly important for exporters and covers bad debt due to default and insolvency;
- legal expenses insurance.

Protection against legal liabilities to third parties

A business has legal responsibilities towards its employees, the public and customers. In addition to the compulsory Employers' Liability insurance, a company can take out insurance for:
- public liability which covers its legal liabilities for death or injury to people and damage to property arising from its business activities;
- product liability which covers damage or injury arising from defects in product design and manufacture.

Personal protection for owners and employees

The temporary or permanent loss of a key person in a business – due to illness, injury or death – can have a significant effect on a business so there are polices which can help reduce this impact. These include:
- personal accident and sickness insurance, particularly important for small companies and the self-employed;
- income protection insurance;
- private medical insurance;
- life insurance and pensions.

3 Read the text and answer these questions.
1 What types of insurance are compulsory for businesses?
2 How can equipment and machinery be insured?
3 Is it possible to insure cash?
4 What is trade credit insurance?
5 Why are product and public liability insurance so important?
6 What personal insurance is important if you work for yourself? Why?

4 🎧 13 Listen to five people talking about insurance. Match each speaker to what he/she is talking about. There are three extra options you do not need.

1 Speaker 1
2 Speaker 2
3 Speaker 3
4 Speaker 4
5 Speaker 5

a ☐ working for an insurance company
b ☐ complaining about an insurance company
c ☐ choosing an insurance policy
d ☐ selling an insurance policy
e ☐ taking out compulsory business insurance
f ☐ criticising the lengthy claim procedure
g ☐ commenting on the cost of insurance premiums
h ☐ taking out business interruption insurance

17th century London marine insurers

Marine insurance

Marine insurance, one of the oldest forms of insurance, can be divided into the following categories for shipowners:
- **cargo** – this specifically insures the cargo of the ship and any passengers' possessions;
- **hull** – the insurance of the actual vessel against damage due to collision, bad weather etc.:
- **liability** – to cover any liability towards any third parties;
- **freight** – to cover the loss of freight money.

Exporters and importers doing international business need to organise their own marine insurance against the risks of loss or damage to their goods in transit, from the time they depart the shipper's warehouse to the moment of delivery at the consignee's premises. There are many different policies, but the main are:
- **voyage policy** which offers insurance cover for one particular voyage;
- **time policy** which is valid for a specified time period, usually a year;
- **valued policy** where the value of the cargo and consignment is indicated in the policy so the amount of any compensation is known in advance;
- **unvalued policy** where the value of the cargo and consignment are not indicated in the policy so the amount of compensation will be agreed after a claim is made;
- **floating policy** where a total insured amount is specified and the details of the ship, voyage etc. are declared at the moment of departure. The policy is open and can continue until the amount is used up. This is the most common policy for companies which make frequent shipments.

5 **Read the text and answer these questions.**

1 What is the difference between cargo and hull insurance for shipowners?
2 Why is liability cover necessary?
3 Why do exporters and importers need to take out cargo insurance?

4 What is the difference between a time and a voyage policy?
5 How do valued and unvalued policies differ?
6 Why is a floating policy most suitable for companies carrying out a lot of shipments?

6 Pairwork **Explain to your partner the importance of insurance for international trade following these guidelines:**

- the purpose of insurance
- obligatory and optional business insurance
- types of marine cargo insurance for international trade

MY GLOSSARY

broker /ˈbrəʊkə/ _____
default /dɪˈfɔːlt/ _____
freight /freɪt/ _____
goods /ɡʊdz/ _____
hull /hʌl/ _____
insolvency /ɪnˈsɒlv(ə)nsi/ _____

insurance /ɪnˈʃʊər(ə)ns/ _____
liability /lʌɪəˈbɪlɪti/ _____
mortgage /ˈmɔːɡɪdʒ/ _____
policy /ˈpɒlɪsi/ _____
risk /rɪsk/ _____
theft /θɛft/ _____

Written orders

An order is a commercial document used to request a company to supply goods or services in return for payment.

A written order can be sent by letter, fax or email. The information that should be included when placing an order is the customer's name and address, a description of the goods and the quantity requested, the price, delivery and payment details. It is also possible to add any conditions the order is subject to.

From: John Wilde <john.wilde@wildeoptics.co.uk>

To: Ken Liu <ken.liu@guangzhoulenses.com>

Sent: 4 March 20..

Subject: Trial order

Attachments:

Dear Mr Liu,

With reference to our previous correspondence, we would like to place a trial order as follows:

Men's sunglasses	No. 4550	100 pieces	@USD 35.00/piece
Women's sunglasses	No. 4580	50 pieces	@USD 42.00/piece
Unisex sunglasses	No. 4600	20 pieces	@USD 50.00/piece

The delivery and payment terms are as per your email dated 27th February 20.. . Please make sure the goods are packed in plywood crates, clearly marked with our company name and address.

We look forward to receiving your pro-forma invoice.

Yours sincerely,
John Wilde

---

1 **Read the email and decide if these sentences are true (T) or false (F). If there is not enough information, choose 'doesn't say' (DS).**

1 John Wilde has done business with this company before. _____
2 He orders a total of 170 items. _____
3 The delivery terms were indicated in a previous email. _____
4 The payment will be made after the goods are dispatched. _____
5 The email contains instructions for how the goods should be packed. _____
6 John Wilde does not request any other documents. _____

2 **Match the two halves of the sentences.**

1 We thank you for	a ☐	your prompt handling of this order.
2 We are pleased to	b ☐	accept these terms, we shall be obliged to cancel our order.
3 We would be grateful if	c ☐	subject to delivery by 18th March.
4 The goods should be	d ☐	place an order for ski clothing.
5 We accept	e ☐	your quotation of 11th September.
6 If you are unable to	f ☐	the payment and delivery terms indicated in your email.
7 Please note that this order is	g ☐	packed in wooden crates and marked with our company name.
8 Thank you in advance for	h ☐	you could offer us a 5% discount on this order.

Order forms and online orders

Orders can also be made by filling in **pre-printed** order forms, and attaching them to an accompanying email, letter or fax, as well as by completing an order form **online**. When ordering goods from a website the whole transaction – the selection of the goods and quantity, authorisation for payment, delivery terms and costs – is usually completed in one go. When you are a registered user of a website, it is possible to store all your details and use a one-click ordering system which makes the process even quicker.

BERTOLUCCI WHOLESALERS

179 West Street

London
NW1 7PL
www.bertolucci.com

Po175 Dried porcini mushrooms 250g pack
Unit Price £17.50

Pa523 Extra long spaghetti 500g pack
Price £1.75

Br556 Bruschetta sauce with basil 375g jar
Price £8.99

Br566 Bruschetta sauce with garlic 375g jar
Price £8.99

Ol987 Pitted black olives in brine 225g can
Price £3.45

Ol997 Whole black olives in brine 225g jar
Price £2.95

CUSTOMER NAME

Nico's Italian Deli
17 New Cathedral Street
Manchester
Tel.: 0161 8956743
Fax: 0161 8956312
Email: gianni@bellaitalia.co.uk

CUSTOMER ACCOUNT

No. 1579

ORDER NO.	897
DATE	8th September 20..
DELIVERY ADDRESS	AS ABOVE

CODE	DESCRIPTION	QUANTITY	UNIT PRICE	TOTAL
(1) _____	Dried porcini mushrooms	(2) _____	£17.50	£262.50
Pa523	(3) _____	12	(4) _____	£21.00
Br556	(5) _____	20	£8.99	(6) _____
(7) _____	Pitted black olives	9	(8) _____	£31.05
			TOTAL	£494.35

3 Look at the order form and catalogue and fill in the missing information.

4 Now answer these questions.
   1 What type of company is Bertolucci?
   2 Who is the client and do you think this is the first time they have ordered from Bertolucci?
   3 What products do they order?
   4 What is the total cost of their order?

Phone orders

Orders can be made by phone directly to the Sales Department of a company. This is common when the customer has some questions to be answered or wants to check availability of a particular product. With phone orders, it is usually necessary to also send a written confirmation.

5 **Complete these expressions with the words from the box.**

> call   catch   deliver   give   place   repeat   sending   take

Checking details
Let me just (1) _____ that to you.
You said model ABC in blue, didn't you?
Did you say 13 or 30?
Sorry, I didn't (2) _____ that.

Placing an order
I'd like to (3) _____ an order.
Can you (4) _____ my order?
I'm phoning to order…

Making requests
Could you tell me if model XYZ is available?
Can you (5) _____ me the item number, please?
Would you mind (6) _____ confirmation by fax?

Making a promise
Don't worry. I'll do it now.
We'll (7) _____ the goods to you by next Thursday.
I'll (8) _____ you back straightaway.

6 🎧 14 **Listen to three customers who call Katie Barnett in the Sales Department of QuikPrint, a supplier of ink cartridges for printers and photocopiers. Complete the missing information.**

QuikPrint Sales Order Memo
Customer: Siobhan, Samuels Ltd
Copier: Xerox (1) _____
Quantity: (2) _____
Price: £(3) _____
Delivery: (4) _____

QuikPrint Sales Order Memo
New Customer: (5) _____ Sykes, Wainwright
Ink cartridges for
(6) _____, model (7) _____
Quantity: (8) _____
Email will follow

QuikPrint Sales Order Memo
Todd Butler from (9) _____ Services
Printer/copier supplies for (10) _____ in the South East
Email with exact (11) _____ will follow
Has requested payment (12) _____ from date of invoice

7 Role play **Practise this phone conversation in pairs. Then swap roles.**

Seller
You work in the Sales Department of Kitchen Maid and you receive a phone call from Kathy's Kitchens. All your items are available immediately except for S124 which will be available in two weeks' time. You deliver by courier all over the country.

Buyer
You work at Kathy's Kitchens, a shop selling kitchen and cooking equipment. You have seen Kitchen Maid's website and would like to place an order. Select the items you wish to purchase from the catalogue and phone Kitchen Maid's Sales Department to place your order.

ITEM NO.	DESCRIPTION	PRICE
S124	20 cm kitchen knife	€23,99
F124	15 cm kitchen knife	€19,99
K178	vegetable peeler	€6,50
M870	lemon zester	€8,25

Accepting or refusing an order

After receiving an order, the seller may acknowledge the order or, under particular circumstances, refuse it. Reasons for refusal can include the temporary unavailability or discontinuation of an item, the impossibility to satisfy delivery deadlines or unacceptable discount or payment requests.

An **order acknowledgement** should:
• thank the customer for the order;
• summarise the details of the order;
• give any necessary explanation, e.g. special discounts, delivery, availability;
• end with a positive reference to this and future business.

A **refusal letter** should:
• refer to the customer's order;
• explain the reasons for the refusal;
• make a counteroffer, if suitable, e.g. offer an alternative item;
• end with a positive reference to future business.

8 **Read these two letters and underline the sentences/parts which correspond to the above points.**

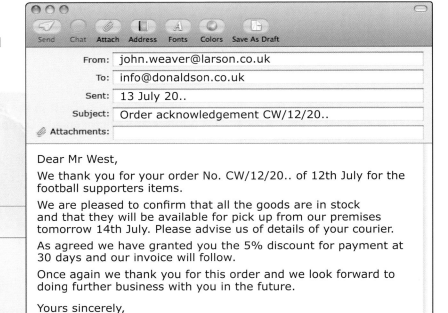

From: john.weaver@larson.co.uk
To: info@donaldson.co.uk
Sent: 13 July 20..
Subject: Order acknowledgement CW/12/20..
Attachments:

Dear Mr West,

We thank you for your order No. CW/12/20.. of 12th July for the football supporters items.

We are pleased to confirm that all the goods are in stock and that they will be available for pick up from our premises tomorrow 14th July. Please advise us of details of your courier.

As agreed we have granted you the 5% discount for payment at 30 days and our invoice will follow.

Once again we thank you for this order and we look forward to doing further business with you in the future.

Yours sincerely,
John Weaver

Café Services
Industrial Park West
Bristol
Tel. 0117 9834210
Fax 0117 9834215

fax

To:	**Anna Jameson**
Fax:	**01494 766523**
Date:	**2nd September 20..**
Subject:	**Your order**

Dear Anna,

Many thanks for your fax order dated 1st September.

We regret to inform you that we cannot process your order in full as, due to an increase in demand, item 105 (Bacon Twists) is currently unavailable.

We apologise for this inconvenience and, as an alternative, we would like to suggest that you try our new Sour Cream and Chive Twists (item 109 in our catalogue) which are extremely popular. For this order, we are willing to offer you 200 packets at the same price as the Bacon Twists.

Please let us know your decision by tomorrow at the latest so that we can guarantee delivery to you by next Tuesday as requested.

We look forward to receiving your reply.

Kind regards,
Andrew Watts

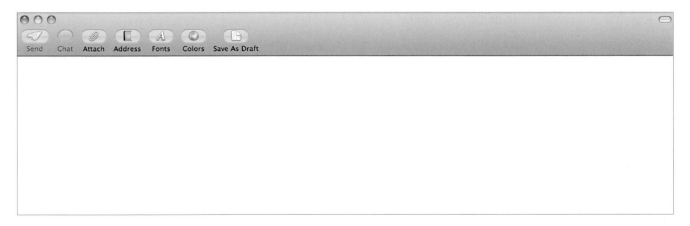

9 **Read the email and put the sentences in the correct order.**

From:	Simon Howard <simon.howard@gseelectronics.com>
To:	Roger Page <r.page@thedvdshop.co.uk>
Sent:	29 October 20..
Subject:	Your order 156/200
Attachments:	

Dear Mr Page,

☐ We sincerely regret any inconvenience and hope to receive further orders from you in the future.

☐ With reference to your above order for 20 portable DVD players, we are writing to inform you that unfortunately we cannot
confirm your order.

☐ In this way we can process your order as quickly as possible.

☐ The expected delivery time would be approximately 6 weeks.

☐ Due to circumstances beyond our control, we are not able to deliver the items within two weeks as requested.

☐ If these terms are still suitable, please let us know.

Yours sincerely,
Simon Howard

10 **Now answer these questions.**

1 What did Mr Page order?

2 When did he want the items delivered?

3 Why can the order not be processed?

4 Does Mr Howard offer an alternative?

11 Writing **Write another letter from Mr Howard to Mr Page (see exercise 9 above) in which:**

- you thank him for his order
- you apologise and inform him the portable DVD model PVP 720 he requests is not in production
- you offer PVP 1020 instead and attach a brochure
- you ask for a confirmation email

MY GLOSSARY

availability /əveɪləˈbɪlɪti/ _____

confirmation /kɒnfəˈmeɪʃ(ə)n/ _____

delivery /dɪˈlɪv(ə)ri/ _____

discontinuation /dɪskəntɪnjʊˈeɪʃ(ə)n/ _____

item /ˈʌɪtəmʔ _____

to acknowledge /tə əkˈnɒlɪdʒ/ _____

to process /tə ˈprəʊsɛs/ _____

to supply /tə səˈplʌɪ/ _____

11 | Trade Legislation and Organisations

1 **Read the text and answer the questions.**

Commercial relations between companies from different countries are regulated by laws. There are local laws set by each country and international laws set by international organisations like the WTO or by groups of countries with a common economic policy like the European Union. The objective of trade legislation is to ensure fair and free trade, which means that the world is seen as an open market where all companies have a right to trade in a correct manner.

Laws regulating trade are of very different kinds. An example of laws that all countries adopt, are those regarding protectionism, that is a set of laws that protects local industries from foreign competition. In other words, these laws restrict international trade in favour of local trade. One of the most commonly used forms of trade restrictions is tariffs – these are taxes imposed on imported goods. The tax makes an imported product more expensive than similar products made in the country.

1 Who can set laws regulating trade? _____
2 What is the objective of trade legislation? _____
3 What is fair and free trade? _____
4 What is protectionism? _____
5 What are tariffs? _____
6 What is the effect of tariffs? _____

2 **Which of these do you think are advantages (A) and disadvantages (D) of tariffs? Write A or a D beside each sentence.**

a ☐ Local companies can compete with foreign companies. *A*

b ☐ Prices are higher for consumers. ____

c ☐ There is no problem of unemployment. ____

d ☑ Competition is reduced so free trade is inhibited. ____

e ☐ Tariffs make governments richer. ____

f ☐ People are encouraged to buy more local products than foreign products. ____

g ☐ There is less choice for consumers. ____

3 🎧 15 **Now listen to two people discussing protectionism and tariffs and number the advantages and the disadvantages in the order you hear them, the first one is done for you.**

4 Speaking **What do you think? Are you in favour of or against protectionism? Choose the arguments from the list in exercise 2. Use these words and expressions below.**

> I'm _____ protectionism.
> I think that / In my opinion…
> First of all…
> Then / Next…
> Finally…

5 Read the text about the WTO and complete the table below.

The WTO (World Trade Organisation) is the most important organisation promoting and regulating free trade in the world. It was created in 1995 and includes 153 member states that meet, discuss trade problems, negotiate and sign agreements. These documents contain the rules for international commerce which all member states must respect. The result of this is that:
- open markets are guaranteed to both producers and consumers
- barriers between people and nations are broken down
- there are common laws that regulate international trade
- importers and exporters are helped in their business

Definition of the acronym WTO	
Date of creation	
Number of members	
Its objective	

6 Read the text again. Can you give a definition of agreement?

_____

7 Read the text and complete the sentences with phrases from the box.

> infringe the law.   trademarks and patents need it.
> examples of Intellectual Property.   inventors and creators.

One of the WTO's agreements is the Agreement on Trade-Related Aspects of Intellectual Property Rights (TRIPS). The basic principle is that ideas and inventions are an important part of trade and must be regulated by common international rules. This agreement protects creators and inventors and gives them the right to prevent others from using their inventions and creations. For example books, films, songs, computer programs are protected by copyright, inventions by patents and brand names and logos can be registered as trademarks. Copyrights do not have to be registered, while patents and trademarks have to be registered in order to receive protection. The symbol for a non-registered trademark is ™, while the symbol for a registered trademark is ®. The registration includes a description of what you want to protect.

1 Copyrights, patents and trademarks are _____
2 The TRIPS Agreement protects _____
3 People who use other people's inventions or creations _____
4 Copyrights don't need to be registered while _____

8 Match the words with their definitions.

1 Trademark
2 Patent
3 Copyright

a ☐ a form of protection of an invention given to the inventor.
b ☐ a form of protection given to authors of artistic works.
c ☐ a word, phrase, symbol or design that identifies a product and belongs legally to its inventor or manufacturer

License to use trademark.
ants to B the sole and exclusive rig

9 How would you protect these? Put them into the correct box.

> a poem   the computer mouse   the logo of an American high school   the lyrics of a song   D&G
> the M in McDonald's   a Maths school textbook   an electric coffee maker   a painting

Copyright	
Trademark	
Patent	

10 Read these situations. What are you infringing? A copyright or a trademark?

1 You go to a concert and film parts of it with your mobile phone. Then, at home, you load it on your blog so all your friends can watch it. _____

2 You buy a fake belt. It looks exactly the same as the original by a famous fashion designer you like but it costs much less. _____

3 You buy a DVD film and make a copy of it for your friend who wants it but doesn't want to spend money to buy it. _____

4 You like the Coca Cola logo. You download it from the Internet and print it on your rucksack.
_____

11 Read this sentence taken from Directive 2006/116/EC of the European Parliament. What does it refer to: copyright, trademark right or patent right? Give reasons for your choice.

> L 372/12   EN   Official Journal of the European Union   27.12.2006
>
> **DIRECTIVE 2006/116/EC OF THE EUROPEAN PARLIAMENT AND OF THE COUNCIL**
> **of 12 December 2006**
>
> The rights of an author of a literary or artistic work (...) shall run for the life of the author and for 70 years after his death.

12 Complete this sentence taken from an Act of the United Kingdom with the missing word.

> A _____ which contains (...) a representation of the Royal crown or any of the Royal flags or a representation of her Majesty or any member of the Royal family (...) shall not be registered unless (...) consent has been given by or on behalf of Her Majesty or (...) the relevant member of the Royal family.

13 Read the text about the EU and find the questions for the answers.

The European Union is a political and economic community of 27 European countries. It was created in 1957 when only 6 countries formed the EEC (European Economic Community) with the Treaty of Rome. Since then, other countries have joined the community and other treaties have contributed to the creation of a community where people, goods and capital can circulate freely. With the Maastricht Treaty of 1992, the European Community became the European Union and the euro was introduced as a single currency which started to circulate in 2002. However, not all member countries have adopted it.

The EU is organised as a single country, so it has a parliament that makes laws that all member countries must adopt.

One of the objectives of the EU is to promote trade among its countries and there are many legislative acts, called Directives, that all member countries must apply. Many of these directives try to protect consumers' rights.

1 _____ ? 27.

2 _____ ? In 1957.

3 _____ ? In 1992 with the Maastricht Treaty.

14 🎧 16 Listen to an expert on EU legislation talking to a group of students about The Toy Safety Directive 2009/48/EC of the European Parliament and complete his talk with the missing words.

We all agree that (1) _____ and games are vital for child development. And we all agree that children must be (2) _____ by laws that guarantee the safety of the toys they play with. We can be sure that toys sold and bought in the European market are subject to a high level of (3) _____.

To start with, let's give a definition of toys. By toys we mean products which are designed for use by children under (4) _____ years of age. There are about 80 million children under 14 in the European Union and about 2000 companies in the toys and (5) _____ sector with about 100,000 people working in the (6) _____,

research, marketing, sales and distribution of toys. 80% of toys in the EU are produced in France, Germany, Italy, Ireland, (7) _____, the UK, the Czech Republic and Poland.

To circulate freely in the European Union, toys must meet the safety requirements shown in Directive 2009/48/EC so that they can be used by (8) _____ with no danger to their health or safety. For example, they must be suitable for the children's age, they can't be inflammable or radioactive and they can't contain chemicals. Also, they must contain warnings, that is notes specifying the limitations of use.

All economic operators are responsible for the toy's conformity: first of all, the manufacturer must declare the toy's conformity and must evaluate the toy's safety before it is put on the (9) _____. In fact, all toys marketed in the EU must carry a CE (which stands for 'Conformité Européenne') conformity marking, which is the manufacturer's declaration that the toy satisfies all safety requirements. Go home and check: you're sure to find the mark (10) _____ on any toys you have. Then, the distributor must verify the toy's (11) _____. These rules are strict for all toys circulating in the EU: this means that they must be applied to toys produced in and exported from the EU and for those (12) _____ from other countries. Our most important partners are the (13) _____ for exports and (14) _____ for imports with 86% of total imports.

Finally, do you know who most toys are bought for in the EU? Infant and pre- (15) _____ children with about 20% of the market.

15 Read the text in exercise 14 and say what these numbers refer to.

1 80 million = number of _____
2 80% = percentage of _____
3 2000 = number of _____
4 86% = percentage of _____
5 20% = percentage of _____

MY GLOSSARY

brand name /brænd neɪm/ _____
copyright /ˈkɒpiraɪt/ _____
to ensure /tuː ɪnˈʃʊə(r)/ _____
fair /feə(r)/ _____
health /helθ/ _____
to infringe /tuː ɪnˈfrɪndʒ/ _____
law /lɔː/ _____
marketed /ˈmɑːkɪtɪd/ _____
patent /ˈpeɪtənt/ _____
policy /ˈpɒləsi/ _____
to prevent /tə prɪˈvent/ _____

protectionism /prəˈtekʃnɪzəm/ _____
research /rɪˈsɜːtʃ/ _____
right /raɪt/ _____
safety requirement /ˈseɪfti rɪˈkwaɪəmənt/ _____
suitable /ˈsjuːtəbl/ _____
tariff /ˈtærɪf/ _____
trademark /ˈtreɪdmɑːk/ _____
trade-related aspects of intellectual property /treɪdrɪˈleɪtɪd ˈæspekts əv ɪntəˈlektʃuəl ˈprɒpəti/ _____
right /raɪt/ _____

12 Marketing

When you buy something, do you ever think about what a company does when it puts a product on the market?

1 Look at this list of steps and put them into the correct order.

- ☐ make the product
- ☐ advertise it
- ☐ distribute the product
- ☐ understand what consumers need or want
- ☐ fix the price of the product at a profit

2 Read the text and answer the questions below.

Today's business world is very complex but the basic principle is still this: companies make products they want to sell at a profit. What makes it complex is that consumers are becoming more and more demanding, and there is more and more competition with other companies which offer similar products so that consumers have a wide range of choice. Therefore companies must plan their activities very carefully: the way they market their products can mean the difference between them and competitors.

Marketing is the process of identifying and satisfying customers' needs. This process must be satisfactory for both sides: for the company because it must sell at a profit and for the consumer because he must be happy with the product so that he will buy it again. Marketing involves different activities. The first one consists of identifying the consumer's needs and wants, that is what the consumer needs and what he wants to buy. This activity involves market research, that is the process of collecting and analysing information about the market for a new or existing product. The objective of market research is to help the company identify the target market, that is the specific consumer group that will buy its product. A company needs to decide this before it starts to produce a product.

There are different methods of market research which can be used: questionnaires, telephone or personal interviews, comments on the Internet. They all consist of questions that give the company information about, for example:

- the customer's profile: his age, interests, lifestyle, etc.
- the features of a product that customers want
- the price they are willing to pay
- the features of a product that they like or don't like
- how often they use and buy a product

Brand Awareness Survey

* What is the first company that comes to mind when you think of goods choice?
* What is the first company that comes to mind when you think of Brand Name manu~~facturer~~?
* How familiar are you with Brand Name man~~u~~
  ○ I've never heard of them
  ○ I've heard of them, but never buy their products
  ○ I buy their products occasionally
  ○ I buy their products on a regular basis
* Which of the following attributes do you associate with Bran~~d~~
  ☐ Essential
  ☐ Fun
  ☐ Modern
  ☐ Affordable
  ~~...~~dable
  ~~...~~ments for Brand Name manufa~~...~~
  ☐ Public
  ☐ Ra~~d~~

1 What is the final objective of any company? _____
2 Why do consumers have a wide range of choice? _____
3 What is the function of market research? _____
4 How can a company carry out market research? _____
5 What do these different methods consist of? _____
6 What type of information can a company get with market research? _____

3 Now read the text again and find definitions for these words:

1 marketing: _____
2 market research: _____
3 target market: _____

4 Royal Sport is a sportswear company. It is now planning to launch a new model of training shoes.
This is the market research questionnaire they have prepared before they start design and production.
What information does Royal Sport want? Match the information to the question numbers from the
questionnaire.

1 Are you   ☐ male or ☐ female?

2 How old are you?   ☐ 15 – 20
                                              ☐ 21 – 30
                                              ☐ 31 – 40
                                              ☐ Over 40

3 How many trainers have you got?   ☐ 1 pair
                                              ☐ 2 pairs
                                              ☐ 3 pairs
                                              ☐ More (please specify number) _____

4 How often do you buy a pair of trainers?   ☐ Once a year
                                              ☐ Twice a year
                                              ☐ Three times a year
                                              ☐ More (please specify how often) _____

5 Are your trainers for a specific sport?   ☐ Yes   ☐ No
   If yes, what sport?   ☐ Tennis
                                              ☐ Football
                                              ☐ Jogging
                                              ☐ Basketball
                                              ☐ Other (please specify sport) _____

6 Where do you buy your trainers?   ☐ Sports store
                                              ☐ Discount store
                                              ☐ The Internet
                                              ☐ Other (please specify place) _____

7 What are the features you look at, when buying your trainers?   ☐ Design
                                              ☐ Price
                                              ☐ Brand name
                                              ☐ Comfort
                                              ☐ Popularity

8 How much are you willing to spend on your trainers? _____

9 Which is your favourite brand of trainers? _____

a ☐ The average age of people who buy trainers
b ☐ What influences their choice
c ☐ If there are more men or more women interested in this article
d ☐ The competitors
e ☐ The place they usually go for their shopping
f ☐ If they wear trainers every day or only when they do sport
g ☐ If their potential customers buys many trainers
h ☐ What consumers think is the right price

5 Choose a popular product you know for each of the product categories in the table below. Then, try to identify the possible consumer profiles for each product, including the information required.

Category	Product	Consumer Profile
Rucksack	_____	Age: Sex: Competitors: Price:
Watch	_____	Age: Sex: Competitors: Price:
Car	_____	Age: Sex: Competitors: Price:
PC	_____	Age: Sex: Competitors: Price:

6 Now, choose one of the products and present your results to the class following these guidelines.

The product I have analysed is _____.
In my opinion, the typical consumer is about (*age*) _____, and usually *male/female*.
I think he/she would find similar products among these brands: _____.
Finally, I think he/she would be willing to pay about _____ euros for this product.

The marketing mix

After selecting its target market with market research, a company must take decisions about the so called marketing mix. This is the combination of 4 Ps:

PRODUCT   PRICE
PROMOTION   PLACE

7 Match the Ps to their definitions.

1 Product
2 Price
3 Promotion
4 Place

a ☐ the distribution of the product
b ☐ the method to persuade consumers to buy the product
c ☐ the type of goods to produce
d ☐ the cost of the product to the buyer

8 What exactly do the 4 Ps involve? Complete with the names of the 4 Ps.

1 _____ involves the money spent by the consumer plus the profit for the company
2 _____ involves how and where consumers can buy the product
3 _____ involves giving the product a name, an image, a design, a packaging, a quality
4 _____ involves deciding how to make consumers know about the product and persuade them to buy it

Product

9 🎧 17 **John Newman works in the Research and Development Department of a company that produces make-up products for teenagers. Listen to him speaking about the importance of packaging in marketing and choose the right options.**

1 If a company wants to sell a successful product, it has to
   a sell it at a competitive price.   b differentiate it from competitors.

2 a Packaging
   b Advertising   plays an essential role in marketing strategy.

3 What attracts a consumer at first is
   a the look of a product.   b the marketing strategy chosen by a company.

4 Packaging   a is simply
                     b is not simply   a container for a product.

5 Packaging helps to
   a protect a product and identify a brand.   b identify a product and sell a product.

Price

10 **Read the text about setting a price for a product and complete the sentences below.**

Setting a price is not easy. If the price is too high, consumers will not buy it. If it is too low, consumers will buy it but the money earned by the company may not be enough to cover the costs. Every company hopes to make a profit. This means that it must be sure that the price is higher than the cost of producing it. However, there are other factors to be considered. For example, it may be useful to see what competitors do: if they offer similar products, their price can be a good starting point. Also, if a company has used market research to ask potential customers what price they are willing to pay for its product, this is another important factor. After setting a product's price, a company may decide to offer discounts which means offering reduced prices to customers who buy large quantities of a product, who pay cash, who buy a product out of season or at the end of a season, that is during sales.

1 Setting a price is not easy because _____
2 The three factors to consider when setting a price are _____
3 A discount is a _____
4 Discounts can be offered to customers who _____

Place

Place refers to the distribution of a product, that is the process of getting a product from the producer to the consumer. Between the producer and the consumer there are intermediaries like wholesalers, who buy from producers and sell to retailers, and retailers who buy from wholesalers and sell to consumers. The majority of consumers buy from retailers, but there are different types of retailers.

11 **Look at the table below and complete it with examples.**

Type of Retailer	Description	Examples
Department store	Large store with different departments for different articles	
Shopping centre/Mall	Many different shops in the same place	
Factory outlet	Store that sells articles from a specific manufacturer at discounted prices	
Specialty store	Store that sells one type of article from different manufacturers at regular prices	
Discount store	Store that sells brand name articles at discounted prices	
Internet	Websites where consumers buy directly	
Outlet	Mall with stores that sell designer articles at low prices	

Promotion

Promotion is the element of the 4 Ps that people associate most with marketing. It is a form of persuasive communication that motivates consumers to buy a product. The most popular methods of promotion are advertising and sales promotions.

Sales promotions

12 Look at these examples of sales promotions and match them with the definitions.

1 free gifts (or freebies)
2 samples
3 coupons
4 buy one, get one free offers
5 loyalty cards

a ☐ certificates that offer discounts on particular products and can be found in newspapers or on the product
b ☐ cards given by stores or supermarkets that give advantages to owners: building up points to get gifts from a catalogue or discounts
c ☐ extra objects included with a product at no extra cost
d ☐ small sized version of a product offered free
e ☐ an offer of getting 2 products for the price of one

13 Look at these pictures and write what types of sales promotions they are.

1 _____   2 _____

3 _____   4 _____   5 _____

14 🎧 18 Listen to Ann Moore, a marketing consultant, talking about advertising and complete the text.

To start with, I'd like to give a definition of (1) _____ and to specify its objectives. Advertising is the process of communicating (2) _____ about a product and of persuading people to (3) _____ it. There are different advertising media with advantages and disadvantages. Let's start with (4) _____ which has a great impact on consumers. TV adverts can be shown several times a day but people can decide not to watch them. Then, (5) _____ or magazines. It is true that they both reach a large number of (6) _____ but the limit is that they are static, so they may have less impact than TV adverts because they don't attract consumers' attention so much. Billboards and (7) _____ displayed outdoors can be effective only if they are (8) _____ but people may not notice them. Finally the (9) _____. Of course advertising over the Internet is the way to reach the largest number of consumers and it has a 'total' impact: sight, sound and motion. But consumers may ignore it and (10) _____ it off.

Internet marketing

Internet marketing or i-marketing has dramatically changed the marketing world. Its ability to identify and target markets at a fraction of what it once cost has made it the ideal tool for any business, be it the largest multinational or a start-up fashion designer selling T-shirts from a basement.

I-marketing can be used to conduct market research and to promote products and/or services in addition to, or as a replacement of, more traditional methods.

Large companies are now using social media like Twitter and Facebook as an extension of their market research department, while small companies rely entirely on these sources to find out what a market wants and what people are willing to pay for a new product or service. Studying Twitter chatter and following Facebook comments have become the new focus groups and consumer panels.

When you use a company app or the 'Like' button on a Facebook page, you are willingly and knowingly sharing your information with third parties. However many internet users are unaware of how much information companies are gathering about us, our habits, lifestyles, likes and dislikes every time we use a search engine, visit a website or click on a link. Cookies, tracking codes and databases are all ways in which a company can track us and store our personal information for later use.

Thanks to these tracking devices, internet ads promoting products and services can be targeted to a specific audience, increasing their chance of success. To reach a wider audience and improve its internet presence, a company can use SEO, while a company blog will help in promoting a corporate image.

15 **Read the text and decide if these sentences are true (T) or false (F). If there is not enough information, choose 'doesn't say' (DS).**

1 I-marketing costs much more than traditional marketing.
2 It is only useful for large multinationals.
3 Social networks have been advantageous for i-marketing.
4 Analysing what people say on social networks is a way of collecting data.
5 All internet users know about tracking devices used to obtain personal information.
6 Cookies are the most common way of tracking internet users.
7 Companies use the information collected by tracking devices to target their advertising.
8 SEO should only be used by companies with high traffic to their website.

16 **Find the verbs in the text for these definitions.**

1 to recognise or distinguish something
2 to select as an object of attention
3 to organise and carry out
4 to learn or discover a fact
5 to collect, group together from different places
6 to follow the trail or movements of someone or something
7 to keep or accumulate something for future use

17 Speaking **Discuss these questions in small groups.**

1 Do you think i-marketing has positive or negative effects for consumers? For companies?
2 Will it replace other market research methods?
3 Do you think it is correct that your internet movements can be tracked? Why/Why not?

MY GLOSSARY

advert /ˈædvɜːt/
to advertise /tuː ˈædvətaɪz/
billboard /ˈbɪlbɔːd/
cash /kæʃ/
to collect /tə kəˈlekt/
coupon /ˈkuːpɒn/
department store /dɪˈpɑːtmənt stɔː(r)/
to earn /tuː ɜːn/
factory outlet /ˈfæktri ˈaʊtlet/
feature /ˈfiːtʃə(r)/
gift /ɡɪft/
interview /ˈɪntəvjuː/
mail /meɪl/

market research /ˈmɑːkɪt rɪˈsɜːtʃ/
to plan /tə plæn/
questionnaire /ˌkwestʃəˈneə(r)/
to reach /tə riːtʃ/
retailer /ˈriːteɪlə(r)/
sample /ˈsɑːmpl/
to set /tə set/
specially store /ˈspeʃəli stɔːr/
target market /ˈtɑːɡɪt ˈmɑːkɪt/
wholesaler /ˈhəʊlseɪlə(r)/
wide range of choice /waɪd reɪndʒ əv tʃɔɪs/
willing /ˈwɪlɪŋ/

13 | Advertising

The purpose of advertising

Advertising is perhaps the most important aspect of **promotion**, the fourth P in the marketing mix, and is used to **persuade**, **inform** and **remind**. It can persuade consumers to buy or use an existing product or service; it can inform them about changes within a company or a new product or service; it can remind them about a company, thus improving its image and building brand identity.

Companies generally divide their advertising into two distinct areas:
- **Business-to-consumer (B2C) advertising:** to persuade the general public to buy the company's products or use its services.
- **Business-to-business (B2B) advertising:** directed at other businesses to inform them about the company and to promote its products and services.

The first thing an advertisement has to do is **to grab our attention** and it can achieve this in a variety of ways: a slogan, a striking image, a catchy jingle or a memorable headline. The second thing is **to provide more information** about the product or service. In a print ad, this will be the body of the ad. The purpose is to create feelings of belief, trust and desire.

The third aspect is to make sure that potential customers can **remember the company or product** and to **reinforce the brand identity**, for example with the logo. The final element, the **call to action**, may be implicit within the ad or specified explicitly, such as inviting viewers to click on a website or visit a store. Since we are surrounded by advertising in all aspects of our lives, we are perhaps becoming more resistant and less open to advertising. Therefore agencies and ad designers have to try to make their ad stand out in a crowd and new advertising models are continuously developed and new media options explored so as to continue to reach the target audience.

1 Read the text and answer these questions.

1 What is the purpose of advertising?
2 What is the difference between B2B and B2C advertising?
3 What are the five things that an advert should do?
4 How can an advert catch our attention?
5 How does an advert try to make us remember a product or company?
6 Do you believe that consumers today are more resistant to advertising? Why/Why not?

2 Match these elements of an advert to the correct definition.

1 slogan
2 image
3 jingle
4 headline
5 body
6 logo

a ☐ the photograph, pictures or other visual elements in an advert
b ☐ the main text of a print ad, with information on the product or service
c ☐ a short, well thought-out sentence, usually the first part of a print ad to be read
d ☐ the unique symbol used by a company or brand
e ☐ a memorable tune or piece of music, mostly used in radio commercials
f ☐ a short, catchy and distinctive phrase to describe a product or a brand

Effective advertising

When creating an advert and defining an advertising campaign, most businesses use the services of an **advertising agency**. Here specialists follow all aspects from the definition of the **USP** (Unique Selling Proposition) and the creation of the ad, to the selection of the advertising media and the length and timing of the campaign.

When creating an ad, agencies and ad designers can try to achieve the objectives of a successful advert – that it should **be noticed, read, believed, remembered and acted upon** – in different ways. They can use a **traditional** approach or try to be more **original**. Both of these have advantages as well as potential drawbacks. Traditional language, images and associations have been tried and tested and are known to work. On the other hand, random or unconnected images, bizarre headlines or invented words can be considered groundbreaking and modern. The downsides are that the first approach may just seem boring and over-used; the second could be too obscure to be properly understood or to catch on.

Humour is another common technique and it is often considered the most successful by consumers and agencies alike, as a funny or entertaining ad is more likely to be remembered.

The use of **famous people** as testimonials can also be considered. A famous actor, sportsperson or model has a very powerful personal image and can bring this to the advert. However, it can be an extremely expensive option and public opinion about who is 'in' or cool can change very fast. Gossip and scandals surrounding a celebrity also risk damaging the company's image.

3 Read the text and decide if these sentences are true (T) or false (F). If there is not enough information, choose 'doesn't say' (DS).

1 Advertising agencies only follow big clients. _____
2 Advertising agencies' services are limited to the creative aspect of an ad. _____
3 A traditional approach to creating an ad does not have any disadvantages. _____
4 An original ad may contain strange or made-up words. _____
5 Both consumers and agencies believe humorous ads to be successful. _____
6 The use of famous people in ad campaigns is in decline. _____

4 🎧 19 **Listen to this manager from an advertising agency talking about creating an effective ad and complete the notes.**

Step 1 – have a clear _____ so your message is focused.
Step 2 – understand the _____ of your ad to make it appropriate and produce results.
Step 3 – show how your product or service will _____ a consumer.
Step 4 – know your USP to define your _____ and use it in your advert.
Step 5 – _____ with the customer, be motivating and encouraging but always believable.

5 Pairwork **Go back to the notes you made about the ads for exercise 1 and discuss these questions in pairs.**

1 Were the ads you remembered more traditional or innovative? In what ways?
2 Did the ads use any humour? If so, do you think it was entertaining or funny?
3 Did the ads feature a famous person? Who? What ideas do you associate with him/her?
4 In general, which of the above-mentioned techniques do you prefer in an ad? Why?

Advertising media

The choice of the media for an advertising campaign depends on several factors, including:
- size, nature and location of the target market;
- the product or service to be promoted;
- what proportion of the target audience will be exposed to the ad;
- the cost.

TV

This is still the most popular choice given its high impact and wide national reach. It is effective for creating brand awareness and selling consumer products. However with the large number of satellite and cable TV channels now available, it is no longer sufficient to advertise just on the top three or four networks, but it is essential to choose the channel and programme with the specific demographic required. TV advertising is extremely expensive, especially for the prime time slots such as early evening or during sporting events, and similarly the investment needed to produce the ad itself is huge. Another downside to TV advertising is that new digital technology allows viewers to skip adverts during playback or viewing, or viewers may just take a break or channel hop during the commercial breaks.

Press

The press has a leading role in advertising campaigns. Printed adverts have the advantage that they can be kept, are often seen repeatedly and can contain more information or details than a TV ad. Their visual impact is still great even without sound or movement. Depending on the target, in an ad campaign it is possible to include international, national and regional newspapers (often a specific section like business, sport or fashion) and general interest or special interest magazines (e.g. computer, sport, hobbies). Naturally, a full colour ad in a glossy magazine is more expensive, and reaches a larger audience, than a black and white ad at the back of a local newspaper.

Radio

This is a cheaper alternative to TV advertising, both to purchase the airtime and to make the ad. It can be national or local but does not reach the same number of people as TV. The creation of the ad has to be carefully considered as it cannot rely on the impact of visual images.

6 Read the texts on these pages and complete this table.

Advertising media	Advantages	Disadvantages
press TV radio outdoor digital media		

Outdoor

Outdoor advertising includes billboards, posters, street furniture and electric signs in public places such as the street, shopping centres, airports, stations and on public transport. Some are much more permanent and have become almost part of the background, while others are changed more frequently, such as on public transport, to maintain impact. The target is the general public, although the location, for example in a football stadium or near a school, can target a more specific market segment.

Digital media

The most rapidly growing sector, Internet, offers targeted advertising worldwide 24/7 with banners, pop up ads, and pay per click advertising, as well as one-to-one emails. Digital advertising is inexpensive, can use sound, visuals and motion to create impact and it is easy to update and evaluate the success rate. A disadvantage is that these ads are very easy for users to ignore while surfing and to delete from their inbox. With social media and apps, advertisers are able to form a more direct contact with consumers, especially young people, creating a global community around a brand or product with consequent positive effects on sales and brand identity. Another advantage of social media is how swiftly messages can be spread. **Viral ads**, for example, can be posted on YouTube or Facebook where they are noticed by net surfers and shared immediately, quickly reaching millions of hits.

7 **Which advertising media do these terms refer to? Now write a definition for each term.**

1 prime time slot _____
2 channel hopping _____
3 glossy magazine _____
4 trade press _____
5 billboard _____
6 street furniture _____
7 banner _____
8 pop up ad _____

8 Speaking **In small groups, discuss which media or mix of media would be most appropriate to advertise these products and services.**

- a shampoo available in supermarkets
- a local repair service for electrical appliances
- a website selling children's toys

- a low-cost dental surgery in your town
- cruise holidays in the Caribbean
- an energy drink

MY GLOSSARY

awareness /əˈweːnəs/ _____
brand identity /brand ʌɪˈdɛntɪti/ _____
promotion /prəˈməʊʃn/ _____

to grab /tə grab/ _____
to persuade /tə pəˈsweɪd/ _____
to reinforce /tə riːɪnˈfɔːs/ _____

14 Bank Systems

Banking can be defined as the activity of accepting or borrowing money from clients, whether individuals or companies, and then lending out this money to other individuals or companies in order to earn a profit. Naturally the services offered by today's banks, as well as the types of bank in existence, are much more multifaceted than this.

Types of bank

Some broad groups of banking categories are as follows:

RETAIL BANKS

These deal with individual customers and concentrate on mass market products such as current and savings accounts, mortgages, loans and credit and debit cards. All of the major four retail banks in the UK also serve the needs of small businesses.

COMMERCIAL BANKS

These deal with business clients, both large and small, and as well as current and deposit accounts, they offer foreign currency accounts and exchange, lines of credit and guarantees for international trade, payment processing, loans for business development and expansion.

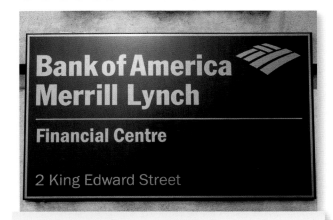

INVESTMENT BANKS

This kind of bank does not take deposits but works with companies and investment markets, for example by underwriting the issue of stocks or bonds and advising on merger and acquisition processes.

PRIVATE BANKS

These manage the banking and financial needs of high-net-worth individuals (HNWI).

OFFSHORE BANKS

These banks are located in countries which are considered tax havens due to low or no tax systems, and they offer financial and legal advantages to investors from other countries.

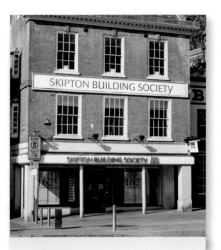

BUILDING SOCIETIES

These are mutual financial institutions, which means that they are owned by their members. In the past their main business was savings accounts and mortgages, although now most have diversified and offer similar services to banks.

POSTAL SAVINGS BANKS

These are operated in conjunction with the national postal system of a country. When they were first introduced, they only offered savings accounts however nowadays most of them offer complete banking services.

1 Read the text and decide if these sentences are true (T) or false (F). If there is not enough information, choose 'doesn't say' (DS).

1 The principal aim of banking is to make a profit through borrowing and lending money. _____
2 Most private customers will have accounts with a retail bank. _____
3 Retail banks do not offer services to any kind of business. _____
4 Commercial banks are bigger organisations than retail banks. _____
5 A company interested in increasing its capital through new shares would consult
  an investment bank. _____
6 Private banks deal with people with a lot of money and investments. _____
7 Offshore banks are only located on islands. _____
8 Building societies and postal savings banks offer similar services to banks. _____

2 Pairwork **Take turns to explain these terms in your own words. Then write the best definition.**

1 borrow _____
2 current account _____
3 lend _____
4 deposit account _____
5 mortgage _____
6 loan _____
7 retail _____
8 profit _____
9 high-net-worth individuals _____
10 tax haven _____

Central Banks

A central bank is responsible for its country's financial affairs and monetary system. Each central bank may have various specific tasks, nevertheless they can be said to have the same main objectives:

- to oversee monetary policy;
- to maintain price stability by controlling inflation;
- to manage the production and distribution of the nation's currency (issue of banknotes and coins);
- to support the nation in times of crisis to prevent its banking system from failing (providing funds to a country's economy when commercial banks cannot cover a shortage);
- to manage interest rates;
- to serve as a banker for other banks.
  It is generally believed that a central bank can carry out these functions if it remains independent from, and uninfluenced by any political regime.

The Bank of England

The central bank of the United Kingdom, known as the 'Old Lady' of Threadneedle Street, was founded in 1694 to act as the bank for the Government and to handle its debts. It has been independent since 1997, after 50 years of nationalisation. Today, its two core purposes are **to maintain monetary stability** and **financial stability**. While the Bank issues the nation's banknotes, it is actually the Royal Mint that produces the coins.

In order to maintain price stability, the Bank's aim is to keep the annual rate of inflation at 2% – the target rate set by the Government – and each month it sets the official Bank interest rate, independently of any Government influence. The Bank works closely with the FSA and the Government to identify and reduce threats, and to maintain the stability of the financial system as a whole. The Bank has recently reviewed its actions and performance during the financial crisis in order to establish ways to improve and reform its interventions for the future.

3 **Read the texts on these pages and decide if these sentences are true (T) or false (F). If there is not enough information, choose 'doesn't say' (DS)**

1 One method of maintaining price stability is to control inflation. _____
2 The Bank of England used to be a nationalised Bank. _____
3 The UK Government decides bank interest rates together with the Bank of England. _____
4 A recent review of the Bank of England found that the Bank had not acted quickly at the start of the financial crisis. _____
5 All of the Federal Reserve is located in the US capital city. _____
6 The US banking system is largely controlled by the Federal Reserve. _____
7 There are many criticisms of the Federal Reserve's monetary policy. _____
8 Eurozone member states no longer have national central banks. _____
9 The national central banks of EU member states have to follow the guidelines for monetary policy issued by the ECB. _____
10 The Eurosystem is responsible for making sure payment systems operate efficiently. _____

The Federal Reserve System

The Federal Reserve System, also known as the Federal Reserve or simply 'the Fed', is the central bank of the United States, founded by Congress in 1913. It consists of a central governmental agency – the **Board of Governors** – in Washington D.C. and twelve **Regional Federal Reserve Banks** located in major cities throughout the United States, each responsible for a specific geographical area and with one or two branches. The Board of Governors' responsibilities include the formulation of monetary policy and the analysis of domestic and international financial and economic developments.
In addition, it supervises the operations of the Reserve Banks and has a significant role in the regulation of the US banking system.

European Central Bank

Unlike other central banks, the European Central Bank, situated in Frankfurt, is not responsible for the banking and financial matters of a single nation, but rather a group of nations. When the first eleven EU member states – and

later six others – adopted the Euro as their single currency, they no longer had monetary sovereignty. However each maintained its own central bank and together these now comprise the **Eurosystem** together with the ECB. The **European System of Central Banks**, on the other hand, includes the ECB and all the national central banks of EU member states whether or not they have adopted the Euro.
According to EU treaty, the basic tasks of the Eurosystem are, among others:
• to maintain price stability;
• to define and implement monetary policy;
• to conduct foreign exchange operations;
• to promote the smooth operation of payment systems;
• to manage foreign reserves of the Eurozone countries.

4 Speaking **Do some further research on one of the above central banks and prepare a short presentation (3-5 minutes). Include these points:**

- its foundation and organisational structure
- its main roles and responsibilities
- any criticisms of its operations, for example, during the latest financial crisis

5 Writing **Does your country have a central bank? What is it called? Write a short presentation text including the following:**

- when it was founded
- what its main purposes and responsibilities are
- where it is located

MY GLOSSARY

bond /bɒnd/ _____
currency /ˈkʌr(ə)nsi/ _____
inflation /ɪnˈfleɪʃ(ə)n/ _____
investment /ɪnˈvɛs(t)m(ə)nt/ _____
loan /ləʊn/ _____
merger /ˈmɜːdʒə/ _____

retail /ˈriːteɪl/ _____
saving account /ˈseɪvɪŋ əˈkaʊnt/ _____
stock /stɒk/ _____
tax haven /taks ˈheɪv(ə)n/ _____
to borrow /tə ˈbɒrəʊ/ _____
to lend /tə lɛnd/ _____

15 The Stock Exchange and How to Read Graphs

1 Read the text about the Stock Exchange and match these titles to the corresponding paragraphs.

> What is a stock/share?   What makes a stock go up or down?
> What is the Stock Exchange?   The risks of investing in shares

1 _____

The Stock Exchange is a place where stocks, also called shares, are traded, that is sold and bought. The most famous stock exchanges in the world are New York, London, Frankfurt and Tokyo. However, stocks can be also traded through the internet. The reason why stock exchanges exist is that companies sell stocks to get money from investors and people buy them to earn money, that is to get money from companies.

2 _____

A stock is a share of ownership in a company. If you imagine the capital of a company divided into equal parts, each part is a stock in the company. So, a stock is part of a company's capital that people can buy.

3 _____

So, now that you have stock and ownership of a company, what can happen? You will make a profit when the price of the stock goes up because you paid a lower price, or you will lose money if the price goes down because you paid a higher price. This means that investing in stocks can be very risky: the hope of making money on your investment does not give you any guarantee that you will make money.

4 _____

Basically, what happens is that if more people want to buy a stock than want to sell it, then the stock's price goes up. On the other hand, if more people want to sell a stock than buy it, then the price goes down because, in order to sell their stocks quickly, they accept a lower price. But what makes people like or dislike a stock?

The obvious answer would seem to be the company's profits, of course. If a company is successful, the value of its stocks will go up. But a stock's performance does not always depend on how well or badly a company is doing. It can simply be determined by the perception, the idea that people have about a company's results. For example, if a company produces a product that is popular and everybody wants to buy it, investors think that the company's profits will go up. On the other hand, if there is a market crisis for a particular product, investors think that the company's profits will go down.

2 Read the text again and find the information.

1 definition of stock exchange
2 definition of stock
3 result of a stock's positive performance for investors
4 result of a stock's negative performance for investors

3 Now use your answers from exercise 2 to make a presentation about 'Investing in the Stock Exchange'.

4 🎧 20 **Listen to Paul Jones, an expert on the stock market, speaking about the reasons why stocks go up or down. Tick (✓) the reasons he mentions from the lists.**

Reasons stocks go up	Reasons stocks go down
☐ growing sales and profits	☐ sales and profits go down
☐ an exciting new product is introduced	☐ a famous investor sells his stocks
☐ the company is bought by another company	☐ a new product is not successful
☐ a great advertising campaign	☐ the company has problems
☐ other companies in the same sector are successful	☐ a competitor introduces a better product
☐ the company starts selling in other countries	☐ other companies in the same sector have a crisis

When you invest in stocks, you will need to understand a stock market table that gives you basic information and price history for stocks to see how a stock is performing, has performed in the past and how its price is changing. You can find them in newspapers or on the Internet. Reading a stock market table is simple once you understand the basic elements it contains.

These two stock market tables refer to Microsoft stocks. The first is taken from the American version of finance.yahoo.com. The second one is taken from a financial newspaper.

1

Microsoft Corporation
(NasdaqGS: MSFT)

Last Trade:	Day's Range:
Trade Time:	52wk Range:
Change:	Volume:
Prev Close:	Avg Vol (3m):
Open:	Market Cap:
Bid:	P/E (ttm):
Ask:	EPS (ttm):
1y Target Est:	Div & Yield:

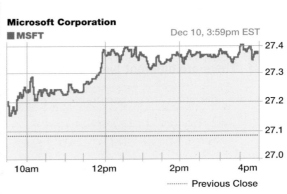

Microsoft Corporation
■ MSFT   Dec 10, 3:59pm EST

2

Company Name	Sales	Hi	Low	Last	Change
Microsoft Corporation	37,629,009	27,40	27,11	27.08	+0.26

5 **The online stock market table and the one from the newspaper look different but the information they give is the same. What do these words from the newspaper correspond to in the online market table? What are the equivalents in your language?**

Newspaper	finance.yahoo.com English	Definition
Sales		
Hi (High)		
Low		
Last		
Change		

6 **Now complete the table in exercise 5 with these definitions.**

the stock price yesterday   total number of stocks traded for the day   the stock's highest price today
the dollar value change in the stock price from yesterday's closing price   the stock's lowest price today

7 **Look at the two Microsoft stock tables and graphs from <u>finance.yahoo.com</u> and find this information. Some parts are highlighted in yellow to help you.**

    1 The date and the time of the stock quotation: _____

    2 The price of the stock on 10th December at 3:59 p.m.: _____

    3 If the price of the stock was different the day before: Yes/No

    4 How much higher today's price is compared to yesterday's: _____ %

    5 The maximum and the minimum prices of the stock today: _____

    6 How many weeks are calculated in a year: _____

    7 The maximum and the minimum prices of the stock this year: _____

    8 The total number of shares traded for the day: _____

    9 The price of the stock at 10 p.m. on 10 December: between _____ and
    _____

    10 The price of the stock at 12 p.m. on 10 December: between _____ and
    _____

How to read graphs

8 **The online Microsoft stock market table includes a graph. What's its function? Tick (✓) the right answer.**

    ☐ To show Microsoft's sales on 10th December.

    ☐ To show the stock's performance on 10th December from 10 in the morning to 4 in the afternoon.

    ☐ To show the value of Microsoft stock on 9th December.

In general, the advantage of presenting data with graphs, charts or tables is that they have a very good visual impact that helps people understand what is being presented in an immediate, clear and easy way.

9 **There are different types of graphs/charts. Look at these and choose their names from this list.**

> bar chart (x2)   line graph   pie chart   pictogram

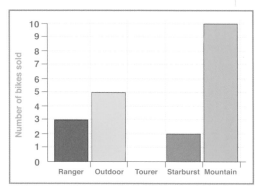

1 _____

2 _____

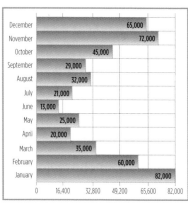

3 _____

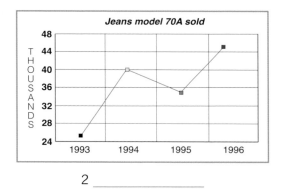

4 _____

5 _____

Presenting a graph involves being able to use a specific lexis.

10 **Look at this table and choose the best alternatives for the descriptions of the graphs in exercise 9.**

Verbs	Nouns	Adjectives	Adverbs
reach a peak go up / increase stabilize go down / decrease	increase / growth decrease / fall	steady gradual slight considerable	steadily gradually slightly considerably

Graph No.3 This graph shows the sales of XY Company in 2010. From January to December sales *decreased / increased* from 82,000 articles to 65,000. From January to April they decreased *gradually / slightly*. In June there was a dramatic *increase / fall* to a value of 13,000. Then, they *went up / went down* again.

Graph No.2 This graph shows the sales of jeans model 70A over a period of 3 years, from 1993 to 1996. The trend was positive because from 24,000 articles, sales *reached a peak / stabilized* to about 45,000. Let's look into details: from 1993 to 1994 sales had a steady *growth / decrease* from 24,000 to 40,000. Then they *went up / went down slightly / considerably* in 1995, but the following year there was a *slight / steady growth / fall*.

11 Speaking **Now, cover up the description of one of the two graphs. Can you describe it in your own words?**

12 **Look at this graph and complete the description.**

This _____ shows the _____ from Sunday 9th May to _____. From Sunday to Monday, sales had a _____ increase from 25 to 28 pieces. Then from Monday to Thursday there was a _____ fall (down to 19 pieces only) but from Thursday to Saturday sales _____ steadily up to 27.

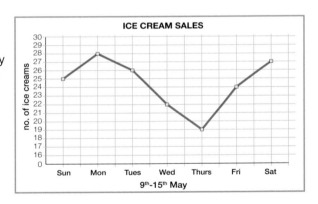

13 🎧 21 **Listen to James Grant describing the sales of CDs in his company over the last five months and draw the line graph.**

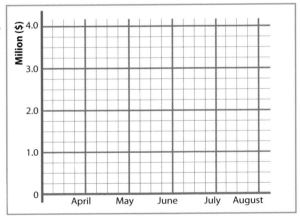

MY GLOSSARY

ownership /ˈəʊnəʃɪp/ _____

performance /pəˈfɔːməns/ _____

share /ʃeə(r)/ _____

stock /stɒk/ _____

to trade /tə treɪd/ _____

Flash on English for COMMERCE
Second Edition

Editorial coordination and project: Simona Franzoni
Editorial department: Pauline Carr
Art Director: Marco Mercatali
Page design: Airone Comunicazione - Sergio Elisei
Picture Research: Airone Comunicazione - Giorgia D'Angelo
Production Manager: Francesco Capitano
Page layout: Sara Blasigh, Federico Borsella

Cover
Cover design: Paola Lorenzetti
Photo: Shutterstock

© 2016 ELI S.r.l
P.O. Box 6
62019 Recanati
Italy
Tel. +39 071 750701
Fax. +39 071 977851
info@elionline.com
www.elionline.com

Printed by Tecnostampa - Pigini Group Printing Division - Loreto, Trevi - Italy
16.83.208.0

ISBN 978-88-536-2179-5

Acknowledgements
Shutterstock, Photos.